DISEASES & DISORDERS

Sexually Transmitted Diseases

DISEASES & DISORDERS

Sexually Transmitted Diseases

Terri Dougherty

LUCENT BOOKS

A part of Gale, Cengage Learning

GALE
CENGAGE Learning™

Detroit • New York • San Francisco • New Haven, Conn • Waterville, Maine • London

LIBRARY OF CONGRESS CATALOGING-IN-PUBLICATION DATA

Dougherty, Terri.
 Sexually transmitted diseases / By Terri Dougherty.
  p. cm. -- (Diseases and disorders)
 Includes bibliographical references and index.
 ISBN 978-1-4205-0220-6 (hardcover)
 1. Sexually transmitted diseases--Popular works. I. Title.
 RC200.2.D68 2010
 616.95'1--dc22
                                                        2009039583

Lucent Books
27500 Drake Rd.
Farmington Hills, MI 48331

ISBN-13: 978-1-4205-0220-6
ISBN-10: 1-4205-0220-4

Printed in the United States of America
3 4 5 6 7 13 12 11 10

Printed by Bang Printing, Brainerd, MN, 3rd Ptg., 12/2010

Table of Contents

"The Most Difficult Puzzles Ever Devised"

Charles Best, one of the pioneers in the search for a cure for diabetes, once explained what it is about medical research that intrigued him so. "It's not just the gratification of knowing one is helping people," he confided, "although that probably is a more heroic and selfless motivation. Those feelings may enter in, but truly, what I find best is the feeling of going toe to toe with nature, of trying to solve the most difficult puzzles ever devised. The answers are there somewhere, those keys that will solve the puzzle and make the patient well. But how will those keys be found?"

Since the dawn of civilization, nothing has so puzzled people—and often frightened them, as well—as the onset of illness in a body or mind that had seemed healthy before. A seizure, the inability of a heart to pump, the sudden deterioration of muscle tone in a small child—being unable to reverse such conditions or even to understand why they occur was unspeakably frustrating to healers. Even before there were names for such conditions, even before they were understood at all, each was a reminder of how complex the human body was, and how vulnerable.

While our grappling with understanding diseases has been frustrating at times, it has also provided some of humankind's most heroic accomplishments. Alexander Fleming's accidental discovery in 1928 of a mold that could be turned into penicillin has resulted in the saving of untold millions of lives. The isolation of the enzyme insulin has reversed what was once a death sentence for anyone with diabetes. There have been great strides in combating conditions for which there is not yet a cure, too. Medicines can help AIDS patients live longer, diagnostic tools such as mammography and ultrasounds can help doctors find tumors while they are treatable, and laser surgery techniques have made the most intricate, minute operations routine.

This "toe-to-toe" competition with diseases and disorders is even more remarkable when seen in a historical continuum. An astonishing amount of progress has been made in a very short time. Just two hundred years ago, the existence of germs as a cause of some diseases was unknown. In fact, it was less than 150 years ago that a British surgeon named Joseph Lister had difficulty persuading his fellow doctors that washing their hands before delivering a baby might increase the chances of a healthy delivery (especially if they had just attended to a diseased patient)!

Each book in Lucent's Diseases and Disorders series explores a disease or disorder and the knowledge that has been accumulated (or discarded) by doctors through the years. Each book also examines the tools used for pinpointing a diagnosis, as well as the various means that are used to treat or cure a disease. Finally, new ideas are presented—techniques or medicines that may be on the horizon.

Frustration and disappointment are still part of medicine, for not every disease or condition can be cured or prevented. But the limitations of knowledge are being pushed outward constantly; the "most difficult puzzles ever devised" are finding challengers every day.

Could It Happen to You?

Maria and Michelle never thought it would happen. Neither thought she was at risk of becoming infected with a sexually transmitted disease (STD). Today they are both living with STDs and coping with the impact of the infection.

An STD is not something that just happens to other people, and it is not something that relates to cleanliness or wealth. Anyone who is sexually active can get an STD. STDs are a serious risk for anyone having sex and are more common than many people think.

Each year 19 million people become infected with an STD. Half of those infected are fifteen to twenty-four years old and may not even be aware that they have come down with an infection that could be a lifelong nuisance or put them at risk of infertility or death.

What Is an STD?

Sexually transmitted diseases, also called sexually transmitted infections, are diseases that can be passed from one person to another through vaginal, oral, or anal sex. Whereas some are easily cured, others are incurable. Common sexually transmitted diseases include chlamydia; gonorrhea; herpes; the human immunodeficiency virus (HIV), which causes acquired immunodeficiency syndrome (AIDS); and the human papillomavirus

(HPV), which causes cervical cancer and genital warts. Syphilis, the oldest known STD, also continues to spread.

Some STD Background

Until the 1990s sexually transmitted diseases were known as venereal diseases. Their name derives from Venus, the Roman goddess of love. Two of the first diseases to be known as venereal diseases were gonorrhea and syphilis. Lesser known diseases such as granuloma inguinale, lymphogranuloma venereum, and chancroid were also some of the first diseases identified as venereal diseases. Today more than twenty diseases are classified as STDs.

A Real-Life Concern

Although STDs are a threat, many teens do not think they are at risk of infection. Anyone who has sex can become infected, however. Susan Cohen has worked in sexuality education for twenty years, and she knows how difficult it is for teens to understand

Many teens do not see themselves at risk of contracting a sexually transmitted disease (STD), but statistics say otherwise.

Chlamydia: Age- and Sex-Specific Rates United States, 2007

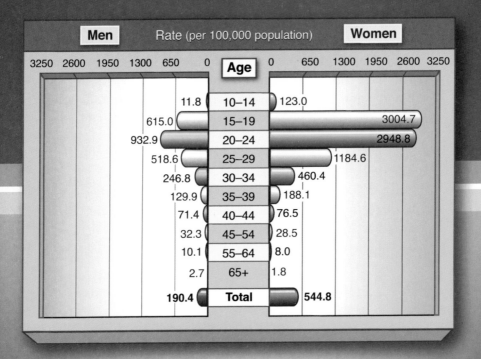

Men	Rate (per 100,000 population)		Women
3250 2600 1950 1300 650 0	**Age**	0 650 1300 1950 2600 3250	
11.8	10–14	123.0	
615.0	15–19	3004.7	
932.9	20–24	2948.8	
518.6	25–29	1184.6	
246.8	30–34	460.4	
129.9	35–39	188.1	
71.4	40–44	76.5	
32.3	45–54	28.5	
10.1	55–64	8.0	
2.7	65+	1.8	
190.4	**Total**	544.8	

Taken from: Centers for Disease Control and Prevention.

that a sexual encounter may have lifelong consequences. "When you're seventeen or eighteen and carefree, you're caught up in what's going on in front of you and it's difficult to see how those decisions you make today, tonight, and tomorrow can affect you years down the line," she says. "But what you do today can affect you tomorrow."[1]

Certain STDs can bring on medical issues that cause infertility in men or women and cervical cancer in women. STDs such as herpes and genital warts continue to plague a person for his or her entire life. In addition, having an STD makes it easier to get HIV, the virus that causes AIDS. The implications of having an STD go far beyond what many people imagine. "There's a financial impact, of treatment, pharmaceuticals, and medical visits; there's the emotional impact to people who are infected," Cohen notes, "and there are obvious relationship, self-esteem, and worthiness impacts."[2]

The Importance of Education

Learning more about STDs can help people make the right choices regarding sexual activity. It can also inform them about how to minimize their risk of getting an STD or giving an STD to another person. "For the most part, people just don't realize how many people have an STD," says Stuart Berman, the chief of epidemiology and surveillance for the Centers for Disease Control and Prevention's STD branch. "It's not a rare event. It's part of being a sexually active person. It's not an issue of it being the nasty kid down the block. The bottom line is, it's very common. It's not somebody else's problem."[3]

CHAPTER ONE

A Significant Problem

The teen came into the doctor's office complaining of severe pain in her stomach. Several tests were done to see what was causing the ache. After scans and scopes failed to show any reason for her pain, her doctor had her tested for sexually transmitted diseases. Finally, the reason for her discomfort became clear. The test for chlamydia was positive. The young woman had caught a common sexually transmitted disease, which led to an infection in her uterus, fallopian tubes, and ovaries, causing the severe pain.

This teen is hardly alone in contracting a sexually transmitted disease. STDs are a major public health concern in the United States. STDs have a significant financial impact, costing the U.S. health care system as much as $15.3 billion each year, the Centers for Disease Control and Prevention (CDC) estimates. "Sexually transmitted infections (STIs), once called venereal diseases, are among the most common infections in the United States today,"[4] notes the National Institute of Allergy and Infectious Diseases.

On the Rise

Many attempts have been made to stop the spread of sexually transmitted diseases, yet these infections remain a major health concern in the United States. John M. Douglas, director

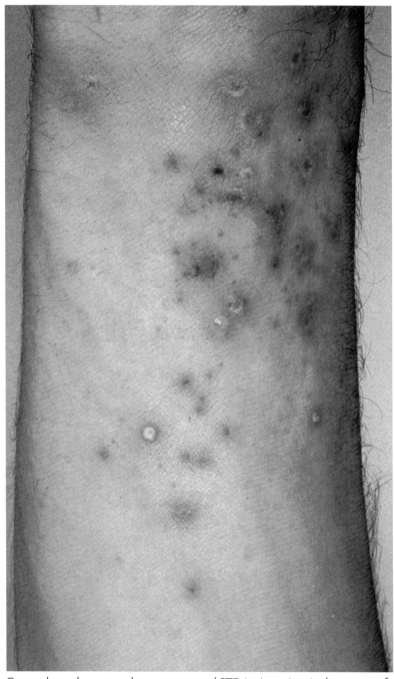

Gonorrhea, the second most reported STD in America, is the cause of these skin abscesses.

of the CDC's Division of Sexually Transmitted Disease Prevention, calls STDs a "substantial threat to Americans."[5] The rates of reported cases of chlamydia and syphilis are on the rise, a 2007 CDC survey shows. The rate of gonorrhea fell 74 percent from the 1970s to mid-1990s, but it is no longer declining. Although the rate has stabilized, the 2007 rate of 118.9 cases per 100,000 people is still well above the U.S. Department of Health and Human Services target of 19 cases per 100,000.

The most commonly reported bacterial infection in the United States is chlamydia. There were 1.1 million cases reported to public health officials in 2007, a number higher than the population of Detroit. The large number of cases of chlamydia set a new record among reportable diseases. "The

Unwanted Trends

The sexually transmitted diseases gonorrhea and syphilis are particularly frustrating to public health officials because their infection rates have stopped declining. Between 1975 and 1997, the number of cases of gonorrhea fell by 74 percent. This was largely due to a gonorrhea-control program that was implemented in the mid-1970s. However, the number of cases has stopped declining and even rose slightly between 2004 and 2005.

Syphilis is another exasperating STD. It has been documented for centuries, and rates hit an all-time low in 2000. Recently, however, the number of syphilis cases has been climbing, and between 2005 and 2006 it increased by 13.8 percent. "The syphilis numbers are real and concerning, not in terms of massive population impact but because this is a disease that had been knocked off its feet—near elimination—and we have seen reverses in what could have been a preventable problem," says John M. Douglas, the director of the Centers for Disease Control and Prevention's Division of Sexually Transmitted Disease Prevention.

Daniel J. DeNoon, "Chlamydia, STD Rates Soar in U.S.," MedicineNet, November 13, 2007. http://medicinenet.com/script/main/art.asp?articlekey-85217.

2007 total represents the largest number of cases ever reported to CDC for any condition,"[6] a CDC report notes. Although the number of reported cases is large, the number of people with chlamydia is even larger. The CDC estimates that less than half of the cases are diagnosed, and that 2.8 million people are infected in the United States each year.

The number of reported cases of syphilis is increasing as well. Syphilis, which is caused by bacteria, has shown a significant decline since the early 1990s and was at an all-time low in 2000. In 2007 the syphilis rate increased 15 percent over the previous year, with more than 11,000 cases reported.

Gonorrhea remains the second most commonly reported infectious disease in the United States. More than 350,000 cases were reported in 2007. The number of actual cases is likely double the number of reported cases, meaning that 700,000 people may be infected each year. The disease is especially common in certain areas of the country. "As in previous years, in 2007 the South had the highest gonorrhea rate among the four regions in the country," the CDC notes. "While the impact is greatest in the South, public health officials have also been concerned in recent years about increases in gonorrhea rates in the West."[7]

Common Concerns

In addition to chlamydia, gonorrhea, and syphilis, other sexually transmitted diseases are common in the United States. As many as 80 percent of adults may be infected with the human papillomavirus (HPV), which can cause genital warts and cervical cancer. The HPV virus often brings people to STD clinics, notes physician Lisa Marr, the author of *Sexually Transmitted Diseases: A Physician Tells You What You Need to Know.*

Genital herpes is another common sexually transmitted disease. Although cases of this disease do not have to be reported to public health officials, it is estimated that one in five adolescents and adults may have genital herpes, which can bring on painful sores. It is caused by the herpes simplex virus type 1 (HSV-1) or type 2 (HSV-2). According to the CDC, at least 45 million people in the United States are infected with one of the incurable herpes viruses.

New Strains of STDs

Many STDs can be easily cured or effectively treated, but in some cases new strains are emerging that make treatment difficult. "The whole reliance on antibiotics in our world has become an issue," says Susan Cohen, who teaches at California State University, Northridge. "We take pills for everything. We're now seeing some antibiotic-resistant strains. Something that might have taken one round of antibiotics may now take two."[8]

One sexually transmitted disease that has become resistant to some treatments is gonorrhea. Penicillin and other drugs were effective treatments at one time, but new strains of gonorrhea are showing up around the world that are not curable by penicillin. In 2006 nearly 14 percent of gonorrhea cases did not respond to traditional drug treatment. Only one class of antibiotics is left to treat these resistant strains, and there is concern that gonorrhea will eventually become resistant to these drugs also. "What would happen if we lost this class of drugs? We would have to turn to classes of antibiotics not previously explored against gonorrhea," John M. Douglas notes. "That might have challenges such as requiring multiple doses or multiple drug combinations."[9]

The Impact on Youth

Although new strains of gonorrhea and the widespread impact of sexually transmitted diseases are of concern to all, today's teens have especially good reason to be concerned about STDs. Though sexually transmitted diseases can affect anyone who is sexually active, they are especially prevalent among young people. According to the National Institute of Allergy and Infectious Diseases, young people aged fifteen to twenty-four account for almost half of all STD cases.

It is estimated that 70 percent of teens have had sex by age nineteen, and 14 percent lose their virginity by age fifteen. The risks of early sexual contact include STDs. "Sex is an emotional decision, a serious decision, and this is another reason to be serious about that decision," comments Stuart Berman, of the CDC's STD branch. He adds that teens need to understand how common and prevalent these infections are, and they need to realize that pregnancy is not the only risk of being sexually active. "It means that sex must not be taken trivially," he says. "It's an important decision. Pregnancy is an important concern, but people also need to be thinking that every time you have sex there's that risk of STDs."[10]

Certain STDs are especially common among young people. According to the CDC, the rate of reported cases of chlamydia is five times higher than that of the general population. "I see mostly chlamydia cases," says Suzanne Swanson, a pediatric gynecologist with ThedaCare in Appleton, Wisconsin, "and the problem with chlamydia is it spreads like wildfire."[11]

A Racial Disparity

Another concern is the difference in STD rates among various races. Some STDs are more commonly found among certain ethnic groups. For example, in 2007 the rate of chlamydia among blacks was eight times that of whites, and the gonorrhea rate was nineteen times higher. In addition, almost 50 percent of chlamydia and syphilis cases are reported among African Americans. "These disparities may be, in part, because racial and ethnic minorities are more likely to seek care in public health clinics that report STDs more completely than private providers," a CDC report says. "However, this reporting bias does not fully explain these differences."[12]

Other ethnic groups also have higher STD rates. The chlamydia rate among Hispanics was three times higher than whites. Among American Indians and Alaska Natives, the rate was about five times higher.

Racial and ethnic minorities may be more likely to get STDs because they often cannot obtain quality health care and thus do not have access to prevention and treatment. "Ensuring that minority communities have access to prevention, screening, treatment and partner services needed to improve health is critical to addressing these disparities,"[13] the CDC notes.

The Impact on Women

Sexually transmitted diseases also hit young women especially hard. Girls age fifteen to nineteen have the highest chlamydia and gonorrhea infection rate of any age or sex group, according to 2007 statistics from the CDC. In addition, a woman who gets the human papillomavirus is likely to contract it in her early adolescent years. About 25 percent of girls aged fourteen to nineteen are infected with HPV, which is the most common virus among teens.

HPV can cause genital warts as well as cancer that forms in the cervix, which is the lower part of a woman's uterus. More than three thousand women die from cervical cancer each year, and about eleven thousand new cases are diagnosed, according to the American Cancer Society. "Having unprotected sex, especially at a young age, makes HPV infection more likely," the American Cancer Society notes. "Also, women who have many sex partners (or who have sex with men who have had many partners) have a greater chance of getting HPV."[14]

One symptom of HPV is the appearance of warts on the body (shown here) and/or on the genitals. HPV can cause cervical cancer.

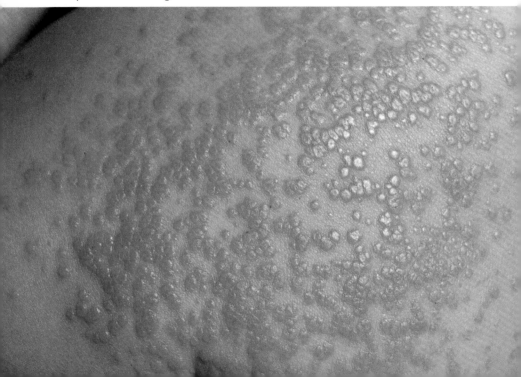

Why Young People?

Young women, age fifteen to nineteen, have a higher rate of sexually transmitted diseases than the general population. According to the Centers for Disease Control and Prevention, this is partly due to the way a woman's body is made. Adolescents and young women are more likely to contract sexually transmitted diseases because the cervix (opening to the uterus) has not fully matured, making them more susceptible to infection. This changes as a woman ages, making her less susceptible to infection.

All young people, male and female, are at higher risk for STDs for other reasons as well. One reason is because they often fail to receive prevention services, perhaps due to a lack of insurance or the inability to pay. A lack of transportation, feeling uncomfortable with testing sites, and concerns about confidentiality are other reasons the CDC notes for higher rates among young people. "Recent estimates suggest that while representing 25 percent of the ever sexually active population, 15- to 24-year-olds acquire nearly half of all new STDs,"[1] the CDC notes.

The choices young people make also play into their high incidence of STDs, notes Stuart Berman of the CDC's STD branch. Teens may be careful to use a condom the first few times they have sex with a partner, but eventually they may lapse. As Berman explains:

> They decide they're in love and can't imagine the person they're in love with being infected and stop using a condom after a couple weeks. That person is just as likely to be infected after a couple weeks as they were when you first met. You really need to use the condom unless you've been tested. All you need is one unprotected exposure. The other four or five times you used protection mean nothing.[2]

1. Centers for Disease Control and Prevention, "STDs in Adolescents and Young Adults." www.cdc.gov/std/stats07/adol.htm.

2. Stuart Berman, telephone interview with author, May 1, 2009.

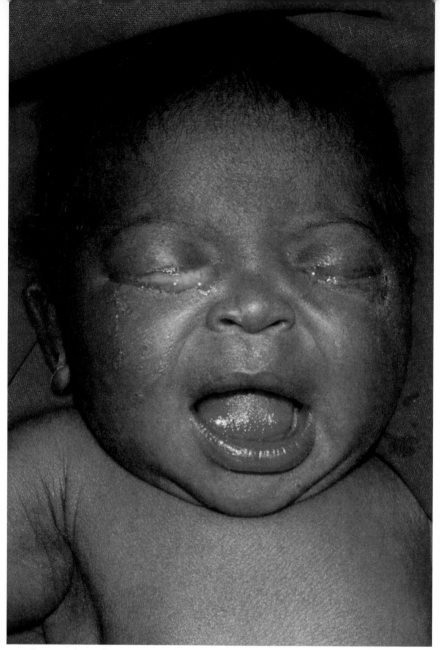

This newborn has an eye infection caused by gonorrhea that was passed on from her mother during childbirth.

Having an STD can also make it difficult for a person to have children. Sexually transmitted diseases are the main preventable cause of infertility, according to the CDC. Up to 40 percent of women with gonorrhea and chlamydia will develop pelvic inflammatory disease (PID), which can damage reproductive organs. According to the CDC, about a million women develop PID each year in the United States. The disease causes an infection in a woman's uterus, fallopian tubes, and/or ovaries. The infection can be treated successfully, but it can cause the fallopian tubes to become scarred. This scarring keeps a woman's eggs from traveling to her uterus, and she cannot become pregnant. "The whole trick is finding that it's there before it's smoldering in there and scarring your tubes," says Jill Grimes, a Texas physician and the author of *Seductive Delusions: How Everyday People Catch STDs*. "We can easily treat the infection once we know it's there, but we cannot treat the scarring that easily."[15]

Issues also arise when a pregnant woman is infected with a sexually transmitted disease. A pregnant woman who has an STD, such as gonorrhea, chlamydia, herpes simplex, or HIV, can pass the infection on to her baby while the child is still in the womb, during childbirth, or immediately after the baby is born. A woman who does not get treated puts her baby at risk for complications. The child may be blind, develop infections, or die shortly after birth. A woman may give birth to a stillborn child, and she may be at higher risk for a miscarriage or delivering a premature baby.

Other Infections

In addition to problems associated with childbirth and a person's reproductive organs, sexually transmitted diseases can lead to infection in other areas of the body as well. In men and women, gonorrhea can spread to the blood, heart, or joints, causing widespread infection and a life-threatening condition. If syphilis is not treated in its early stages, it can bring about serious long-term complications in men and women. Late-stage syphilis can cause brain damage, cardiovascular and other organ damage, and death.

Sexually transmitted diseases can also lead to infertility in men. For instance, bacteria from the STDs chlamydia and gonorrhea can cause epididymitis, which is a painful infection in the tissue around the testicles. It can be treated with antibiotics, but the disease can bring on scarring that may lead to infertility.

Increasing the Chances of HIV Infection

Another serious concern is that a person who already has a sexually transmitted disease is more likely to also become infected with HIV, the incurable virus that causes AIDS. A woman who has chlamydia is five times more likely to get HIV from someone infected with the virus than a person who does not have chlamydia. A person infected with syphilis increases his or her risk of getting HIV two to five times, according to the CDC.

A person with an STD has a higher chance of getting HIV because the STD breaks down the body's natural barriers that provide infection protection. The sores and microscopic tears and skin abrasions associated with many STDs make it easier for HIV to enter the body. "It's like when you have allergies and your respiratory tract is irritated so you're more likely to catch a cold,"[16] explains Grimes.

The Emotional Impact

In addition to the physical impact of an STD, there is an emotional toll. When Anthony L. Contreras, of Los Angeles, learned he tested positive for HIV, he could not think straight. "There was this wave of shock that kind of paralyzes you, then there's a flood of different thoughts that go through your mind lightning fast," he says. As the reality of the disease set in, he began to doubt his self-worth. "There's a feeling of being damaged goods, a feeling you'll never be loved," he says. "Are people going to judge me? Turn their backs on me?"[17]

Being diagnosed with an STD can bring on feelings of being alone and unwanted. It is not unusual for a person to experience shock and dismay at such a diagnosis. "When a person finds out she has genital warts it can be devastating," notes Grimes. "They think, 'How would anyone ever want to be with me?'"[18] When Maria, twenty-four, learned she had herpes at age twenty-one, she sat in her room, crying in disbelief. "There was a feeling of 'Who's going to want me now?' There was embarrassment." It wasn't until she went to counseling that she began to heal emotionally. "It helped me realize that I'm not the only person out there with an STD,"[19] she says.

Some STDs can be easily treated, while others can be readily controlled.

Although it is unsettling to be diagnosed with an STD, a person can learn to live with the disease. Some STDs can be easily cured, and incurable ones can be managed through treatment. "Getting [an STD] does not mean your life is over," Berman notes. "Getting it does not mean you're damaged forever."[20] Michelle Landry, who learned she had herpes at age thirty, was initially shocked by the diagnosis and went through a period of depression. Eventually she came to realize that she is not defined by the disease. "I did not want to live in fear or shame," she says. "I saw other people who had let it affect their lives. What it comes down to is that I'm the same person I was before I had herpes. I'm still as funny, as funky, as witty, as eclectic, except now I have herpes and it's manageable."[21]

Being diagnosed with an STD can be a wake-up call, making a person more responsible about his or her decisions regarding sexual activity. It often makes a person lose the feeling of invulnerability and realize that he or she is not immune, notes Cohen. "STDs have a huge emotional impact on young people," she says. "Unfortunately, it's that first STD that really gets a person to slow down and say, 'This can really happen to me.'"[22]

CHAPTER TWO

Diagnosis, Testing, and Treatment

Sometimes sexually transmitted diseases announce themselves loudly, producing sores or other symptoms that clearly indicate a problem. Other times they whisper their presence, with hints that something is not quite right. And sometimes, an STD remains completely quiet, present in the body but not displaying any signs or symptoms that show it is there.

Because not everyone with an STD experiences telltale signs of an infection—and because symptoms may be confusing—a test may be the only way for a person to know whether he or she has an STD. Some sexually active people may wonder why they should bother getting tested if they show no symptoms, but early detection can help them avoid severe complications down the road. If left untreated, STDs can eventually cause problems such as infertility or cancer. A person can also infect others even though no symptoms are present.

Easy and painless tests can check to see whether a person has an STD. Many STDs are curable, and they are easiest to treat if found early. If a person is found to have an STD that is incurable, it can still be treated to make it more manageable.

Symptoms

When a person has become infected with an STD, sometimes visible symptoms make that infection apparent. Symptoms of

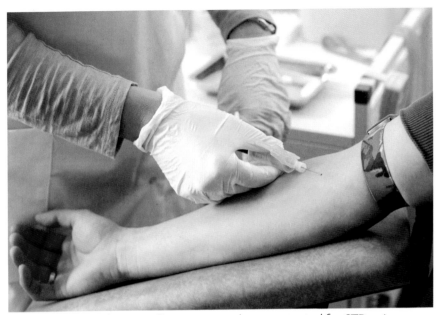

It is important for sexually active people to get tested for STDs, since some symptoms are difficult to interpret and others may be undetectable.

various STDs include warts, blisters, painful urination, or unusual discharge. The lymph nodes may also swell when a person has an STD. Lymph nodes are small, bean-shaped organs that are found at various places in the body. They are part of the body's immune system and help fight infection. When a person has an STD, nodes in the neck, armpits, and groin may swell. Swollen lymph nodes, however, may also be an indication of an illness that has nothing to do with an STD; therefore, a person should check with a doctor for the cause of this symptom.

One warning sign that should always be checked out by a doctor is unusual discharge from the vagina or penis. The STD chlamydia, for example, may cause a woman to experience abnormal vaginal discharge. Gonorrhea may also cause a woman to have a yellowish discharge. Although it is not uncommon for women to have some clear, odorless discharge from the vagina, if it starts looking different or there is pain, odor, or itching to go along with it, she should see a doctor.

Discharge is also a symptom of STDs in men. A man with chlamydia may have discharge from the penis (usually seen in the morning, before he goes to the bathroom for the first time). The STD gonorrhea may also cause discharge that is white, yellow, or green. "Discharge from the penis is never a normal occurrence, and any man experiencing this symptom should be examined by a health care provider while he is having this symptom,"[23] notes physician Lisa Marr.

Other STD symptoms in men can include burning with urination, pain, itching, and irritation inside the penis. These symptoms either may be constant or may come and go, and they indicate that a man should see a doctor.

In both men and women, certain sexually transmitted diseases may cause sores or bumps to appear on a person's genitals. Genital warts are one of the most common symptoms of an STD. These flesh-colored bumps on the skin, which are caused by certain strains of the human papillomavirus (HPV), are harder than

These genital warts were caused by the human papillomavirus.

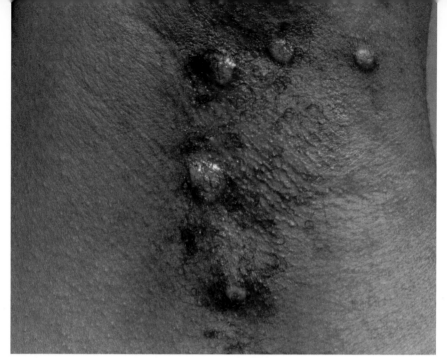

This secondary syphilis infection has spread to the armpit. Syphilis symptoms are ofen indistinguishable from those of other diseases.

the surrounding skin and can be flat or raised. Few or many bumps may appear, and they can be small or large in size. Herpes may also announce itself with red bumps or pimplelike bumps in the genital area. Classic genital herpes lesions are painful blisters or ulcers on the genitals. In some cases, people with gonorrhea also notice sores in the genital area, where painful pimples may appear. Although a rash in the genital area may be a sign of an STD, it may indicate an unrelated infection. "When a person notices a rash, sores or lesions, he or she should see a health care provider as soon as possible after symptoms start, since the appearance of a rash may change over time, and seeing the rash as soon as possible helps the health care provider make the correct diagnosis,"[24] Marr notes.

Sometimes an STD causes an infection that is not in the genital area. A person who performs oral sex is at risk for getting gonorrhea or chlamydia in the throat. Syphilis can also be transmitted during oral sex. A sign of this infection could be a sore throat, although many other infections also cause this symptom.

A person may also show symptoms of an STD on the anus. Sometimes this is because the infection spreads there from another infected area, and sometimes the infection occurs because of anal sex. A woman can get an anal infection if she has an infection of the cervix or urethra and the infected secretions spread. Symptoms of an anal infection can include severe pain and discharge. Bleeding and difficulty having a bowel movement may also occur.

"Silent" Diseases

Although symptoms such as warts, blisters, or discharge may be signs that a person has a sexually transmitted disease, it is possible to have an STD without showing any symptoms at all. It may also take years for symptoms to present themselves. For these reasons, some STDs are called "silent" diseases. A person may have them, and infect others, without realizing it. However, just because a sexually active person does not show signs of having an STD does not mean he or she is not infected.

The signs and symptoms of STDs can also be the same as the signs and symptoms of other illnesses, sometimes making it a challenge for doctors to diagnose them. Syphilis, for example, is called "the great imitator" because its symptoms often mimic the symptoms of other diseases. People may not realize that their sores are due to syphilis during the disease's first and second stages. A person may have the disease for years and not know it.

Pelvic Inflammatory Disease

Sometimes a sexually transmitted infection is not noticed right away and the infection spreads. When it spreads to a woman's reproductive organs, the impact is serious. The infection can cause a painful condition called pelvic inflammatory disease.

Two common causes of PID are chlamydia and gonorrhea; almost half of women with untreated chlamydia develop PID. The bacteria from these STDs cause inflammation of the cervix, and this then spreads to the uterus, fallopian tubes, and ovaries. According to the Centers for Disease Control and Prevention, about one million women develop PID each year in the United States. It is the cause of infertility in ten thousand women each year, as PID can scar the fallopian tubes and block the release of eggs. It can also lead to tubal pregnancy, a life-threatening condition in which a fertilized egg grows outside the uterus, usually in a fallopian tube. A woman with PID may also have pelvic pain that is chronic and long-lasting.

The most common symptom of PID is pain in the lower abdomen that is usually felt as a dull ache. Other symptoms can include pain during intercourse, abnormal discharge, spotting between periods, heavier-than-usual periods, chills, fever, and nausea. Because the symptoms of PID may be mild and vary from person to person, it can be difficult for a health care provider to diagnose. Once a diagnosis is made, PID can be treated with antibiotics.

PID is an especially troubling issue for young women. About three-quarters of the women who get PID are under age twenty-five, possibly because women in this age group are more likely to practice unsafe sex and be exposed to partners who are infected with the bacteria that cause PID. A person who has sex with multiple partners increases her chances of getting PID, and a woman who has had it once is at higher risk of getting it again. "A single episode of PID changes the anatomy of the pelvic organs, so that a woman is at higher risk for developing PID again if she is infected with this bacteria,"[25] Marr notes.

The Progression of STDs

It is not only women who may become infertile if chlamydia or gonorrhea progresses to a more serious infection. Men run the risk of getting epididymitis, an infection that can lead to infertility.

Epididymitis is an inflammation of the epididymis, which sits above the testicles. Signs include discharge and burning with urination, swelling, and pain. The swelling and pain usually occur on one side. Other signs may be that half the scrotum is swollen, hot, and painful. The infection can be treated with antibiotics.

Other STDs can progress to serious conditions as well. Syphilis is curable, but if it is not treated it can bring about serious long-term problems. These complications include brain, cardiovascular, and organ damage as well as death.

A sore in the early stages of the disease can progress to a rough, reddish rash, which may not itch. Other symptoms of

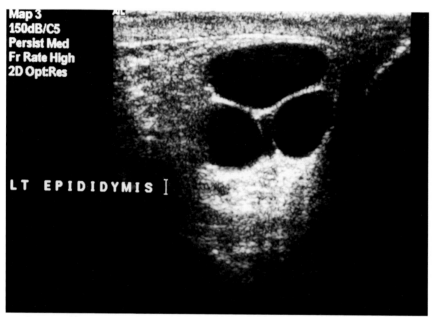

Map 3
150dB/C5
Persist Med
Fr Rate High
2D Opt:Res

LT EPIDIDYMIS

Pictured here is an ultrasound scan of epididymal cysts (three black areas, center) on the testicle of a forty-two-year-old man. The cysts are fluid-filled sacs that form along the epididymis, a coiled tube that stores and carries sperm from the testicles.

the second stage of the disease can include fever, swollen glands, a sore throat, and fatigue. The symptoms of this stage of syphilis will go away without being treated, but that does not mean that the disease is gone. Without treatment, syphilis progresses to its latent stage, in which the disease may hide for years. The infection is still in the body, however, and can progress to the late stages of the disease, which can cause serious medical problems such as damage to a person's brain and heart as well as blindness, dementia, and paralysis.

The virus that causes genital herpes can also go into a latent state. The herpes simplex virus (HSV-1 or HSV-2) is still present in the body during the latent state, but it does not produce infectious particles. Over time the number of outbreaks a person experiences may decrease, but this does not mean that the body is free of the virus. Another outbreak of sores may occur at any time and usually appear during times of stress.

Although outbreaks of herpes are considered more of a nuisance, another STD that can progress to a life-threatening stage is HPV. Some subtypes of HPV can lead to cervical cancer in women, which is a serious condition. In some cases, the cells that line the cervix divide and grow wildly, bringing on cervical cancer. The cancer goes through several stages and can be found early through a screening called a Pap test.

STD Testing

Having a regular Pap test can help a woman discover whether the cells in her cervix are changing and becoming cancerous. Catching the disease early gives a woman a better chance of successfully treating it. Likewise, tests for other STDs give a

Having Symptoms?

A person should see a doctor if he or she has discharge, burning during urination, or an unusual sore or rash. If these symptoms occur, stop having sex and seek treatment. A person who has been diagnosed and is being treated for gonorrhea should tell his or her sex partner about the diagnosis so he or she can also seek treatment. Telling that person can help stop the spread of the disease and prevent that person from developing serious complications if the disease is not treated. While being treated for gonorrhea, it is important to avoid having sex.

Even if you are not showing symptoms, it is a good idea to be tested for STDs if you are sexually active. If you are having sex with a new partner, doctors recommend getting a checkup within a few months to make sure you have not acquired an STD. "Young men tend to only see a doctor when they have symptoms, but both genders, and especially young women, often have no signs when they're infected with an STI," notes Glenda Newell of Planned Parenthood Golden Gate in San Francisco.

Melissa Daly, "Choose a Checkup," *Human Sexuality Newsletter*, December 2008, p. 1.

person a good chance of detecting the disease early and receiving proper treatment.

Even without the visible signs of an STD, a person can carry the disease in his or her body and still may be able to spread it to others. For this reason, testing is necessary. Urine tests, blood tests, and swab tests are all used by doctors when testing patients for STDs.

A urine test, for example, is used to see if a person has chlamydia. A person gives a urine sample, and it is examined in a lab for signs of chlamydia bacteria. A urine test may also be used to see if a person has gonorrhea.

Some clinics and doctors' offices can do a Gram stain to test for gonorrhea. This test, which works better for men than women, involves taking a sample from the urethra or cervix. The sample is placed on a slide and is stained with dye before it is examined under a microscope. A doctor then looks for bacteria in the sample.

A swab test is another test that can be used by doctors to check for chlamydia and gonorrhea. With a swab test, a sample is taken from the cervix, penis, or other infected area. The sample is then analyzed in a laboratory.

If a patient's symptoms include sores, a sample may be taken from a sore to test for the STD. A health care provider will usually diagnose herpes in this manner. A person can also be tested for syphilis by having a health care provider take fluid from a syphilis sore and test it.

A blood test is another tool doctors use to screen for certain STDs. A blood test can be used for both HIV and syphilis. The blood test can detect antibodies that the body produces after a person is infected.

Who Should Get Tested?

The tests for STDs are not complicated for health care professionals to perform, and it is recommended that a person who has sex with more than one partner be tested for STDs. People should also get tested if their partner is having sex or has had sex with others. A positive test allows a person to get treated and helps halt the spread of the disease.

Getting tested for an STD can also be good for one's mental well-being. Testing may put a person's mind at ease, as sometimes what appears to be an STD is not. "Occasionally people will think they have herpes or warts and it's not," says Grimes. "There are a lot of benign bumps on penises that have nothing to do with disease, but don't ignore them. Find out one way or another."[26]

Treating Curable STDs

With a positive STD test result, a person may learn that the infection is very easy to treat and cure, or he or she may find out that more extensive treatment is needed. Two common STDs, chlamydia and gonorrhea, can be successfully cured with antibiotics. A single dose is often all that is needed to cure them. Many people who have gonorrhea also have chlamydia and can take antibiotics for both diseases simultaneously.

In some cases, gonorrhea may be more difficult to treat, however. A person who has a strain of gonorrhea that is resistant to some classes of drugs can work with his or her doctor to find a medication that works. To help prevent the disease from becoming resistant to more drugs, a person being treated for gonorrhea should take all recommended medication.

It is easy to treat and cure syphilis when the disease is in its early stages. To treat the disease, a person receives an intra-

Because an STD can easily be passed from one person to another, both people in a relationship should be tested.

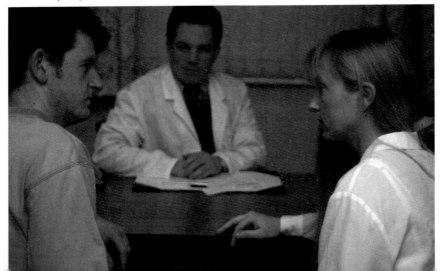

muscular injection of penicillin from a health care profes-
sional. The duration of treatment varies, depending on the
stage of the disease. For people who have had syphilis for
longer than a year, more doses of penicillin will be needed. If a
person is allergic to penicillin, other antibiotics are available to
treat the disease. The treatment kills syphilis bacteria and prevents further damage. However, if a person's brain, heart, or
other organs have been damaged by syphilis, it will not repair
the damage that has already been done by the disease.

Treating Incurable STDs

Some STDs cannot be cured, but they can often be controlled
with medication. Genital herpes is one STD for which no cure
exists. However, people with herpes can take medications
that make outbreaks of the sores shorter and can even prevent
them in some patients. The treatment differs for the first time
a person has a herpes outbreak, for an acute outbreak, and for
long-term suppression of the disease. A person who has more
than six occurrences in a year may benefit from taking medication daily to suppress the virus.

HPV, which causes genital warts and can lead to cervical
cancer, also can be treated but not cured. A person who gets
genital warts can treat them with a medicated cream or can
have them surgically removed through freezing or burning.
Genital warts often go away on their own, although the virus
remains in a person's body.

Genital warts are only one condition brought on by HPV,
which has more than one hundred subtypes. Although some
subtypes cause no health problems, others cause genital warts
or cervical cancer. Certain types of HPV bring about cervical
cancer when they cause abnormal cells to divide and grow out
of control at the opening to the uterus. If the disease is caught
early, 92 percent of people survive for at least five years after
the cancer is found. Treatment for cervical cancer depends on
the stage of the disease. Common treatments include surgery,
radiation, and chemotherapy.

Another STD that can be treated but not cured is HIV,
which attacks a person's immune system and causes AIDS.

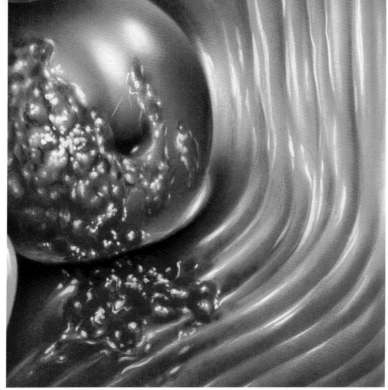
Computer artwork of cancerous cells on the cervix and vaginal wall is shown here. Four thousand women die of cervical cancer each year in the United States.

HIV is constantly changing and quickly becomes resistant to drugs. However, there is medication to slow the progression of the disease. Today, treatments for people with HIV allow them to live longer than they would have been able to in the past. Nonetheless, HIV remains a major health threat in the United States.

Avoiding Reinfection

Sometimes a person who has received treatment for a curable STD will continue to experience symptoms or test positive for the STD. This means the person has been reinfected. The curable STD, such as gonorrhea or chlamydia, was likely cured the first time, but the person has become infected with it again.

To prevent reinfection, a person's sex partners should also be treated for the STD, even if they do not show symptoms. A person should abstain from sex until treatment has ended. If a person has an STD, there is a good chance that his or her partner has it also. "If one person in a partnership is infected, there is more than a 50 percent chance the other partner is infected,"[27] notes Berman.

If symptoms do not go away within one or two weeks after a person has finished taking medication, he or she should see the doctor again. The Office on Women's Health, part of the U.S. Department of Health and Human Services, also advises women to be retested for chlamydia three or four months after receiving treatment. This is especially important if a person's sex partner has not been treated or if a person has sex with a new partner. The test will ensure that the woman gets proper treatment if she has become reinfected.

In its early stages, syphilis is easily treatable with penicillin injections.

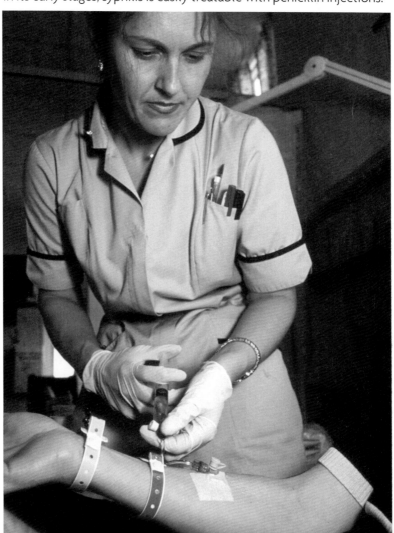

If Your STD Test Is Positive

If you are diagnosed with an STD, it is your responsibility to tell your last sexual partner about the STD and abstain from sex during the treatment process. Telling your partner about the infection builds a trusting relationship and lets him or her know that it is time to get tested. "Being diagnosed with an STD does not mean that you are a bad or immoral person," says physician Lisa Marr. "STDs are caused by germs with which people can become infected while having sex. Some are curable, some are not."[1]

Talk to your doctor about what it means to have an STD. It is not unusual for a person diagnosed with an STD to feel emotional, but your doctor can help you understand your treatment options and how this will impact your life. Parents can also be a source of support. Notes physician Jill Grimes, "I have yet to have a parent who lit into their kids for this situation. Recognize that your parents are human and have [also] made mistakes. Take ownership for your actions and your parents will respect you more for telling them so they can get you some help. Your parents want what's best for you."[2]

1. Lisa Marr, *Sexually Transmitted Diseases: A Physician Tells You What You Need to Know*. Baltimore: Johns Hopkins University Press, 2007, p. 291.

2. Jill Grimes, telephone interview by author, April 14, 2009.

It is especially important for women to be retested after receiving treatment because serious problems can develop if a woman is reinfected. A woman who is reinfected is at a higher risk for reproductive health issues, including infertility.

Because early treatment is so important to curing and controlling sexually transmitted diseases, it is important for young people who are sexually active to get tested for STDs. The simple tests can help avoid more serious problems later on and can save others from becoming infected. As Berman notes, "This is a case of sometimes what you don't know can hurt you."[28]

CHAPTER THREE

People Living with STDs

No one plans on getting a sexually transmitted disease or having to cope with the emotional and physical implications one brings. Yet millions of people are impacted by various STDs and the changes they produce in their lives. Statistics and clinical information about the signs and symptoms of STDs can make the problem seem distant and unreal, but behind these numbers are real people who must deal with the implications of STDs as they go on with their daily lives. STDs can bring on physical challenges as well as feelings of fear, uncertainty, and dismay, but they can also be something a person learns to live with and accept. The infections impact people from all walks of life, and each person reacts to the disease and copes with it in his or her own way.

Maria: Living with Herpes

Sexually transmitted diseases were the farthest thing from Maria's mind when she felt an attraction to a good-looking guy in one of her college classes. She was always happy when he would meet her and her friends out at popular nightspots. Before long it became apparent that the attraction was mutual.

One night they went home together. One thing led to another, and they had sexual intercourse. They used protection, and Maria had no concern that their night together would lead to a

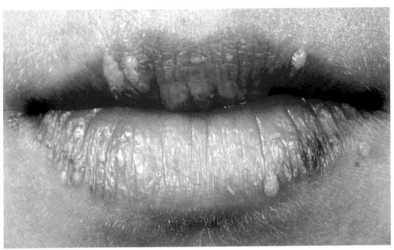

Herpes simplex cold sores are shown on a teenager's lips.

sexually transmitted infection. She never thought that night would be the beginning of a lifelong herpes infection for her.

Maria had no idea that her partner had herpes or that she could get the genital herpesvirus even if her partner used protection. (The herpesvirus can spread if the sores are not covered by a condom and can also spread even if the sores are not present.) "I was twenty-one and you think you're invincible," she says. "I hadn't been promiscuous. It can happen to anyone and that's why I wanted to share my story."[29]

Several days later Maria realized something was wrong. When she went to the bathroom, it hurt to urinate. Her joints got sore, and her knees ached. "I could barely walk down stairs," she says. "I was in excruciating pain."[30]

When she felt a tingling in her genital area and saw the sores, she knew she had become infected with herpes. The signs were readily apparent. "I didn't even really need to go to the doctor, but I did," she says. "I went to an urgent care clinic, and she did a biopsy of a sore."[31]

A few days later the doctor called to confirm Maria's suspicions. Even though Maria had already known in her heart that this was the case, the emotional impact of hearing that she indeed had herpes was horrible. "I was beside myself," she says.

"I cried; I sat in my room and balled my eyes out for a good amount of time. I could not believe this was happening to me. I thought, 'Who's going to want me now?' There was such a feeling of embarrassment."[32]

Maria needed someone to confide in, and she turned to her mother for support. She told her about her condition and the pain she was having. Together, she and her mother went to see Maria's gynecologist to find out what could be done.

Maria learned that her condition could not be cured, but medication could make the outbreaks less severe. She began taking a medication called Valtrex, and she continues to take it every day to suppress the effect of the infection. "Some people take it only when they're having an outbreak coming on," Maria says. "I wanted to avoid it altogether."[33]

In addition to Valtrex, Maria has found lysine tablets can help shorten the duration of the outbreaks. She also learned that stress and a lack of sleep can bring on an outbreak. As a college student, she did not always get enough rest, but she did her best. "The first outbreak was probably one of the worst; they've gotten better since then," says Maria, now twenty-four. "The first year was pretty hard. I probably had one outbreak a month. Now it's very mild, more of an inconvenience."[34]

Whereas medication has helped make Maria's physical symptoms less severe, seeing a therapist has helped make living with the disease less emotionally painful. The therapist emphasized to Maria that she is far from the only person who has the infection. Maria also realized that her fear that no man would ever find her attractive was unfounded, and she entered into a stable relationship.

Because of her initial emotional distress and fears, Maria wanted to tell others what her experience has been like. The disease can happen to anyone, she notes, no matter how careful he or she may be. "I wanted to share my story because . . . there's a stigma," she says. "I've told a couple of my closest friends, and they say you never would think that would happen to you, you're so careful."[35]

Maria still knows people who do not use protection and do not seem to be worried about catching an STD. She wants them to realize that the threat is out there, even though it is not openly discussed often enough. "People don't talk about it, and the doctor made me realize that it happens more often than not, unfortunately,"[36] Maria says.

Kelly: A Regular Mom

Kelly is thirty-six years old, the mother of a two-year-old with another baby on the way, and has been dealing with herpes for twenty years. The infection is part of her life, but she has not let it hold her back from having a happy marriage and family life. "It happened and I'm dealing with it," she says. "Everything is going well. I sometimes forget that I even have it."[37]

Because she takes precautions, Kelly is not worried that her herpes will have an impact on the health of her children or husband. She has not let it control the way she lives her life, and this includes the way she has approached pregnancy and childbirth. When she prepared to give birth to her first child, she talked with her doctor about what she should do so she could give birth vaginally, rather than by cesarean section, to avoid the risk of transmitting herpes to her baby. A mother having a herpes outbreak at the time of delivery risks infecting the child, so to reduce this chance Kelly took daily medication forty-five days before her due date to lessen her risk of having an outbreak. When the day of her daughter's birth arrived, Kelly was not having an outbreak and was able to give birth vaginally. Her daughter was not infected and remains healthy. Kelly plans to have a vaginal birth for her second child also, unless an outbreak occurs shortly before her baby is due to arrive.

Kelly's husband also remains uninfected. They do not use condoms, but they abstain from sex when she feels an outbreak coming on. "It's being honest. If I feel a little of a sensation that may be an outbreak, I'm going to play it safe so I don't get my partner sick," she says. "Sometimes it turns into nothing, but I'd rather be safe than sorry."[38]

Herpes has been such a common part of her life for so long that she was shocked when a teenage female relative was not supported by her parents when they learned she had herpes. The girl and her family were broken up about the disease, Kelly says, and were also misinformed about the implications of the disease, telling the girl that having herpes would negatively affect any romantic relationship she ever has. The young girl was also embarrassed by her partner's sharing the news of her infection with others at their school, and she was scared rather than comforted by her parents because of their misunderstanding about the disease.

Their reaction and lack of knowledge about the disease prompts Kelly to stress that a person with herpes is not defined by the disease and can have a rich and fulfilling life. "Yes, I regret that I have this but it hasn't ruined my life," she says. "It's really important for a young person who may feel self-conscious or vulnerable to have good access to information about what this means in their life."[39]

Gathering information about the condition helped Kelly deal with herpes after she was diagnosed with the disease. She was twenty and in college when she learned she had genital herpes, but the news did not scare her as she already suspected that something was amiss. "I wasn't shocked or depressed because, maybe without even knowing it, I had been dealing with it for a couple years,"[40] she says.

If a pregnant woman is experiencing a herpes outbreak, she can pass the virus on to her baby during childbirth.

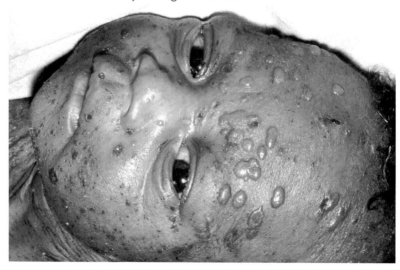

She suspects she became infected while she was in high school. At age sixteen she was in a steady relationship. Because she was using birth control, she felt it would be all right to have sex without a condom. As far as Kelly knew, the relationship was monogamous, but she later learned her boyfriend had been having sex with another girl. While in high school, she broke out with painful blisters on her genitals, a symptom of herpes. "Shortly after I found out that he had been spending time with someone else, I had my first outbreak," she says. "It was a typical first outbreak, very painful, but I didn't know what it was and it went away."[41]

Complications for Babies

Babies whose mothers have sexually transmitted diseases are at risk for many life-threatening problems. Mothers can pass STDs on to their children during pregnancy or childbirth.

A pregnant woman with chlamydia, for example, may pass her disease on to the baby during childbirth. This can result in the baby's getting an eye infection that can cause blindness if untreated. A newborn can also contract pneumonia, characterized by congestion and a cough that worsens.

A pregnant woman who has gonorrhea is at risk for miscarriage or delivering a preterm baby. A baby infected with gonorrhea can become blind or have a joint or blood infection. The blood infection can be life threatening.

If a pregnant woman gets herpes, the infection can be fatal to her baby. Likewise, a pregnant woman who has syphilis puts her baby at risk for complications ranging from developmental delays and seizures to death. The baby may die shortly after birth, or a woman may give birth to a stillborn baby. An infected baby may be born with no signs of the disease initially, but after a few weeks he or she can develop serious problems if not treated immediately. Because of the severe complications that can occur, it is recommended that every pregnant woman be tested for syphilis.

Those with herpes must be open and honest with a potential partner and must also take care to use a condom.

The disease did not flare up severely enough to cause her to seek medical treatment for several years, and after she was diagnosed, Kelly was determined not to infect anyone else. If her boyfriend had been honest with her, she reasoned, she could have been spared the sometimes painful condition. She learned more about the infection and made sure anyone she became romantically involved with was also educated. She was honest about her condition, made sure her partner used a condom when they had intercourse, and did not have intercourse when she had an outbreak or suspected one was coming on. Kelly explains:

> I got pamphlets and brochures to help understand it. Anytime I was spending time with a man and thought there was the potential for romantic involvement, I had this brochure I would give him. I would tell him that I had herpes, and that I understood if the information scared him. I would give him the brochure and let him read it. No one freaked out, no one was scared by it or really weirded out

by it. Open communication has helped me avoid getting other people sick.[42]

Kelly has come to terms with living with her condition and what she must do to keep from infecting others. Although having herpes is not an ideal situation, she wants others to know that a person with a herpes infection can live a normal life. "Herpes has not negatively affected [my life] in any major way," she says. "It's almost like a nonissue."[43]

Michelle: Living with the Impact of HPV

Michelle did not know what the human papillomavirus (HPV) was when she was in high school. She did not realize that HPV would lead her to develop cervical cancer and ultimately take away her ability to become pregnant.

Michelle had her first sexual experience at age fourteen, not realizing that sex put her at risk for getting HPV, which can lead to cervical cancer. "At such a young age we don't know all the facts or consequences," she says. "I can't say who I got HPV from and it doesn't matter, but I do know that at sixteen I went to the gynecologist for the first time, and at seventeen I had a second Pap test and had an abnormal Pap."[44]

The Pap test checks for changes in the cells of the cervix, which is in the lower part of the uterus. Cells in the cervix may change from normal to precancerous and then to cancerous, and a Pap test is done to see if any changes are occurring. The abnormal cell growth is caused by HPV.

Michelle was found to have abnormal cells in her cervix. To remove them, her cervix was frozen to kill the abnormal cells through cryosurgery. "After that they followed me pretty closely," she says. "I had Pap tests every three months for a year, and then every six months for another year."[45]

The Pap tests were done to screen for more abnormal cells, and after two years of normal Pap tests she went back to having an annual screening. Then, at age twenty-five, Michelle began to notice itching in her genitals. A biopsy showed that she had a precancerous condition of the vulva, a woman's external genitals. The precancerous condition can be caused by HPV. To

Cervical Cancer

About eleven thousand new cases of invasive cervical cancer occur each year in the United States, according to the American Cancer Society (ACS). Although the disease causes almost four thousand deaths each year, it is curable when found and treated early. A Pap test is used to detect cervical cancer in its early stages; because of this lifesaving screening, the number of deaths from cervical cancer has gone down.

The cervix is located in the lower part of a woman's uterus. It connects the uterus, which is where a fetus grows, to the vagina, or birth canal. According to the ACS, cervical cancers usually begin with precancerous changes to cells in the cervix, and it usually takes several years for them to develop into cancer. The precancerous cells may go away without treatment, but they may turn into an invasive cancer. Treating the precancerous cells can prevent almost all true cancers.

To avoid getting HPV, the American Cancer Society recommends the following guidelines:

- Delaying sex. "Waiting to have sex until you are older can help you avoid HPV," the society notes.
- Use condoms. "Condoms cannot protect completely against HPV," explains the ACS, "but they also protect against HIV and some other sexual diseases."
- Do not smoke. According to the ACS, "Not smoking is another important way to reduce the risk of cervical pre-cancer and many other cancers."
- Get the HPV vaccine. "There are now vaccines that can protect people against certain types of HPV," the society says.
- Have a screening to find precancerous cells before they can turn into cancer. The Pap test is the most common.

American Cancer Society, "Can Cancer of the Cervix Be Prevented?" www.cancer .org/docroot/CRI/content/CRI_2_2_2x_Can_Cancer_of_the_Cervix_Be_Prevented .asp?rnav=cri.

treat the condition, the abnormal cells were burned off of the vulva during laser surgery. "It was extremely painful," Michelle says. "Today I know that the cell changes were the direct result of the HPV infection, but at the time I wasn't educated enough to know that."[46]

The next year, during a routine exam, she was tested for HPV and also had a Pap test to check for abnormal cells in her cervix. Although the Pap was normal, she tested positive for a type of HPV that is linked to cervical cancer. Additional exams and biopsies revealed that she had cervical cancer. Michelle researched her options and had surgery that would remove her cervix but still leave her with a chance of having children one day. The surgery was successful, and for two years Michelle's cancer went into remission.

Three days after her boyfriend proposed, however, Michelle had another checkup and learned that her battle with cancer was not over. The cancer had returned, and she would require more surgery. "I went from the highest high to the lowest low in the universe,"[47] she says.

She knew she would need to undergo surgery and other treatments for her cancer. Still hoping to have children, she underwent a procedure that removed some of her eggs from her ovaries. Ten days after getting married, she had surgery to remove her uterus and other reproductive organs. To kill the cancerous cells, she also had radiation and chemotherapy.

The cancer treatment was not easy on Michelle. The chemotherapy made her feel nauseated, and it made her feel queasy just to smell food cooking. The radiation was even harder on her body. Her husband comforted her by simply rubbing her feet or head while she had her chemotherapy treatments. "It was a crazy experience, but it taught me what real love is about," says Michelle. "Sex is something we do, but there are so many other ways you can be intimate and show somebody you love them."[48]

While she was in college, Michelle had written a research paper on cervical cancer. It was around this time she had her first cancer surgery, and she was amazed to find how little people knew about HPV and cervical cancer. "I was utterly amazed at the lack of knowledge," she says. "They hadn't heard of HPV. Most of them had no idea of the risk factors."[49]

That is when she decided she would not keep her cancer a secret and would use her story to try to educate other women. She now speaks to groups about cervical cancer and has a Web site with information on the subject, MichelleLeeWhitlock.com. The Tennessee woman, now thirty-four, is the director of the Mid-South Chapter of the National Cervical Cancer Coalition.

With the help of a surrogate mother, she was able to have a child. It has been a long and painful road to motherhood for her, and she wants others to know the implications of STDs. "These STDs are so rampant that you can have sex one time, with or without a condom, and you can get HPV or genital herpes and it will change your life forever. You cannot take it back," she says.

> You always think it's going to happen to that girl, you know the one, the promiscuous girl, the one from the wrong side of the tracks, the one from the wrong neighborhood. It doesn't matter how pretty you are or wealthy you are or what family you come from, it happens to people from all walks of life. The truth is you can come from the best family, or be the smartest girl in school and you can still be that girl.[50]

Anthony: The Emotional Impact of HIV

When he was first diagnosed with HIV, there was no way Anthony could stop thinking about the disease. The reality was with him when he woke up, all through the day, and into the evening. Even if he wanted to try to forget for a little while, his pill regimen of two in the morning, two at midday, and two more before bed brought him back to reality.

"It was the first thing I had to think about in the morning and the last thing I had to think about before going to bed," he says. "It didn't allow me the chance to feel normal, which is, I think, what everyone wants."[51]

It took two years for Anthony to come to terms with his HIV-positive status. He eventually realized that he was much more

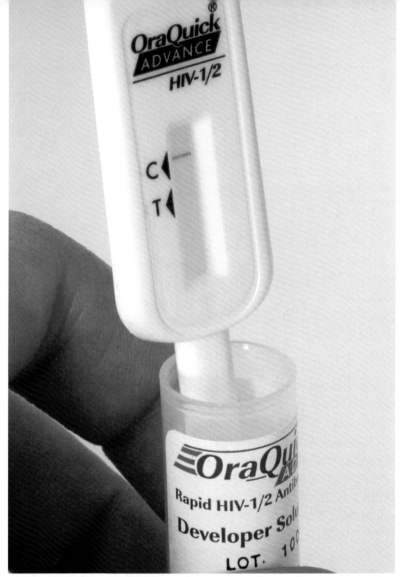

HIV tests, such as OraQuick, can be purchased over the counter, and test results are available in about twenty minutes.

than simply a person with HIV and that he had much to offer. But before he began feeling worthy again, he went through a period of depression that made it a struggle just to get out of bed in the morning. He felt unloved and unwanted. "I was looking for love and acceptance and value, and I couldn't find it,"[52] he says.

Anthony gradually began to see himself as a person, not a virus. He got a job educating others about HIV and its prevention. When he talks to young people about the disease, however, he is sometimes surprised by the many misperceptions he encounters. Some worry that it can be transmitted through sweat (it cannot), and others think that girls do not get it (they can). Most unsettling is the notion he encounters that HIV is no longer a big deal because there are drugs and treatments for it, although Anthony knows all too well that the disease is incurable. "That's the difficult part, trying to make them see that there still is risk involved,"[53] he says.

Anthony is well aware of the risk of having unprotected sex, even one time. At age twenty-one he had sex for the first time and insisted that his partner use a condom. His partner refused. Finally, Anthony gave in.

A few months later, Anthony realized something was not right when he became very sick. The next time he became ill he went to a doctor and asked to be tested for "everything." "He asked if I was at risk for HIV, and I said yes," Anthony says. "He told me he had done hundreds of these tests and only two had ever been positive, so I didn't think anything about it that weekend. Then I got the call on Tuesday, and the doctor said the results showed that everything came back fine except for the HIV, which was positive."[54]

For a time, Anthony did not know what to think. His mind was flooded with thoughts as he wondered how this disease would impact his future and how he would ever tell his family. By now, his former partner wanted nothing more to do with him. "At twenty-one it was a slap in the face," Anthony says. "Sex is a very harsh world."[55]

Anthony came to realize that he could not let the virus overtake who he was as a person. He saw value in sharing the message that an HIV-positive person is so much more than simply someone with HIV. The virus does not change the fact that someone is still someone's son or daughter and has many valuable gifts to offer. "You are not a virus; you are a person,"[56] he says.

For the past decade, Anthony has lived with acceptance of his condition. Now thirty-four, he is proud of the work he does in HIV education and is supportive of the young people he meets and educates. "You really build this relationship and rapport with these kids who are looking for guidance and acceptance; just take an interest in them and care,"[57] he says.

He still sees room for improvement, however, when it comes to dealing with people who learn they have HIV. "What is really missed and left out is the emotional strain it puts on you," he says. "There's a feeling you're damaged goods, a feeling you'll never be loved. Are people going to judge me? Turn their backs on me? Nobody thinks about any of that." There are implications of having HIV that people do not think of, he says, if they focus on treatment of the virus alone. "Even if there is treatment and education, there are other things factored in that you don't account for," he says. "How do you date somebody? I've been on a lot of really good first dates, but when it gets to the end of the night, I was getting, 'You should have told me sooner,' and that's really damaging."[58]

A message that teens often miss, he says, is that sex has implications. Teens often underestimate the risk of getting an

The Human Immunodeficiency Virus

The human immunodeficiency virus (HIV) is the virus that causes AIDS. AIDS is fatal if not treated. According to the Centers for Disease Control and Prevention, more than 1 million people in the United States have HIV, but 20 percent do not know they have the disease. In 2006 more than 56,000 people became infected with the disease.

HIV can be passed from person to person through blood, semen, preseminal fluid, vaginal fluid, or breast milk.

Certain groups have a higher risk of acquiring HIV. Gay and bisexual men have higher HIV rates than heterosexual men. Black men and women and Hispanic men also have higher HIV rates than other ethnic groups.

STD, he says, and they also do not realize what a serious decision it is to have sex with someone. "You're opening the door not just to the emotional aspect of sex," he notes, "but all the disease that comes with it."[59]

Tom: Pain Every Day

A diagnosis of herpes can be unsettling and disturbing news, bringing emotional pain that exceeds the physical discomfort the disease causes. Tom, a fifty-six-year-old father of two, has been troubled and distressed since recently learning he was infected with genital herpes.

When his doctor first told him he had herpes, Tom could not believe what he was hearing. "I went to the doctor because I had what I thought was a callus," he says. "It looked like a callus to me. Then he ran the test and it wasn't a callus." The doctor explained that the herpesvirus could have been dormant for years, appearing when triggered by stress or some other factor. "At first I didn't believe it, I just couldn't believe it," the Iowa man says. "I went through the denial period and then I went through the blame period."[60]

The fact that he has likely had herpes for years without knowing it was also upsetting for him. He believes it to be the result of a relationship he had more than a decade earlier when he was separated from his wife. After that relationship, he and the woman he had been involved with were both treated for chlamydia, which was quickly cured with an antibiotic, but he was not tested for other STDs. Tom's relationship with the woman ended, and he returned to his wife. For a while he was afraid to have children because he feared he had another sexually transmitted disease.

After no symptoms appeared, he thought everything was fine. He and his wife had another child, and Tom stopped thinking about sexually transmitted diseases until the sore appeared.

The infection has not bothered him much physically. Medication taken when an outbreak begins controls the symptoms. The emotional aspect of the diagnosis is another matter, however. "It's been more of a mental thing than a physical thing," he says, noting that it is an unpleasant reminder of the separation from his wife. "I feel it's affected my relationship with my wife and my family," he says. "My wife says I'm not as loving as I used to be, not as touchy feely."[61]

The diagnosis is something he has not told others about. He cannot bring himself to mention it to his wife for fear of re-opening the wounds of their previous separation. "I'm afraid if she gets tested she's going to have it," he says. "She's going to blame it on me, and that thing from ten years ago will pop back up. I'm afraid it will ruin my marriage if I bring it up." As he keeps the information inside, however, there is no denying that it is an uncomfortable secret he is keeping. "It's on my mind every day," he says. "Every day."[62]

CHAPTER FOUR

Causes and Prevention

The existence of sexually transmitted diseases and what causes them is no secret. Scientists have long known that the rashes, discharge, and sores people develop because of STDs are mostly caused by microscopic organisms that enter a person's body or live on the skin. It is also well known that STDs are spread through sexual contact.

Yet STDs continue to spread, and new infections occur every day. This is because the reason for the spread of STDs goes beyond scientific knowledge of bacteria and viruses. It also has to do with people's attitudes toward sex and the information and misinformation they have about sexual contact.

Risky Business

Sexually transmitted diseases do not discriminate. They can impact anyone who has sex, from the richest person on the block to someone struggling to pay for lunch. Your neighbor, boyfriend, girlfriend, brother, or sister could have an STD or have been treated for one.

Although any sexually active person can become infected, a person's decisions can put him or her at higher risk for getting an STD. A person who has sex—either oral or vaginal—without using a condom is at higher risk for an STD. People are also at higher risk of getting an STD if they have sex with someone who has sex with others.

Certain lifestyle choices increase a person's risk of getting an STD. A woman is at a higher risk if her boyfriend has had sex with other men. Another group that is at high risk for STDs is men who have sex with other men. Others at risk include people who inject drugs, people who have been diagnosed with other STDs, and prostitutes. The people at highest risk of getting an STD are those having sex with a prostitute as well as those sharing needles during intravenous drug use.

Mixing drugs, alcohol, and sexual behavior is a dangerous business, as using drugs or drinking alcohol increases a person's risk for getting an STD. Because drinking and drugs impair judgment and decision making, a person under their influence may do things that he or she normally would avoid. "People partying under the influence is a big issue," says Susan Cohen, who works in sexuality education. "Maybe some of the safer sex guidelines they set for themselves are in their head somewhere, but when they're partying those guidelines are nowhere to be found."[63]

What Causes STDs?

Although certain lifestyle choices put a person at higher risk of getting a sexually transmitted disease, the diseases themselves are caused by an infection. Sexual contact allows the infection to pass from one person to another. This infection can be carried by bacteria or by a virus living in certain body fluids. When a person has sex, these fluids are shared and the infection is spread.

Bacteria are the cause of STDs such as chlamydia and gonorrhea, which can be treated and cured. The gonorrhea bacteria thrive in the warm and moist areas of a person's reproductive tract. The bacteria can easily grow in a woman's cervix, or opening to the womb; a woman's uterus, or womb; and fallopian tubes, or egg canals. It can also grow in a man's urethra, which is the urine canal. When a person has sex with another person who has gonorrhea, these bacteria are passed from one person to another.

The bacteria can be passed from one person to another through vaginal, oral, and anal sex. Bacteria living in a man's

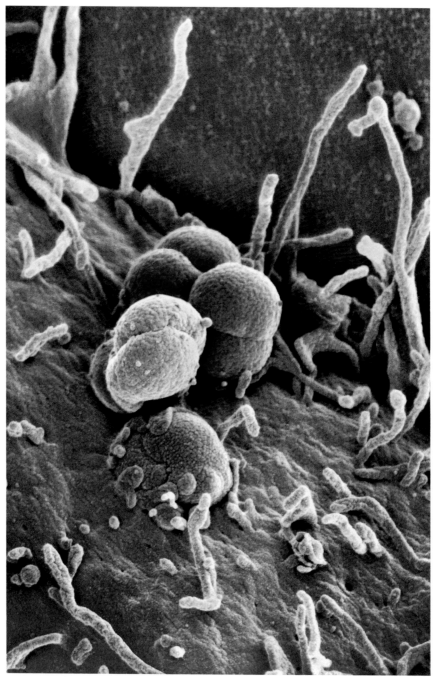

A colored scanning electron micrograph shows gonorrhea bacteria (blue) infecting a human epithelial cell (purple).

urethra can be transferred to a woman's vagina during sex, and they can also be transferred to a person's anus during anal sex. It is also possible to catch a sexually transmitted disease through oral sex, as the bacteria living in a man's or woman's genitals can be transferred to a person's mouth. A sexually transmitted virus can also be spread this way. Although some people consider oral and anal sex to be safe ways to have sex, this is not true. STDs can easily be spread through any kind of sexual contact. "All sex is sex and is a way you can acquire sexually transmitted diseases," notes Stuart Berman. "The infection is a bit different, the implications are a bit different, but lots of kids are appalled to learn they can get gonorrhea of the throat, and they can get syphilis orally."[64]

Syphilis is another sexually transmitted disease that is caused by bacteria. This disease is highly infectious, and a person gets it by coming into direct contact with a syphilis sore. These sores are usually on the outside of a person's genitals, the anus, in the rectum, or in a woman's vagina, but they can also be found on the lips and mouth. When a cut or the mucous membrane of the vagina or anus comes into contact with the syphilis sore, a person becomes infected with syphilis.

Viral STDs

Chlamydia, gonorrhea, and syphilis are caused by bacteria, but other well-known STDs are caused by viruses. These microscopic organisms live and reproduce inside host cells. An STD caused by a virus can be treated but not cured.

One STD caused by a virus is herpes, which can be caused by herpes simplex virus type 1 (HSV-1) or herpes simplex virus type 2 (HSV-2). The herpes simplex virus is the cause of cold sores as well as genital herpes.

HSV-1 is typically associated with cold sores. The majority of people come into contact with this common and highly contagious virus as children, through kisses from friends or relatives. Between 50 and 80 percent of adults have HSV-1, and the American Social Health Association estimates that as many as 90 percent have it by age fifty. The virus typically causes redness, bumps, or blisters on the lips or inside the mouth that heal within a few days.

Most cases of genital herpes are caused by HSV-2. A person can get genital herpes through sexual contact with someone who is infected with the virus. Although the majority of genital herpes is caused by HSV-2, it is possible for HSV-1 to also cause genital herpes. A person who has HSV-1 in the mouth can infect a person's genitals through oral sex. People can also get HSV-1 or HSV-2 through genital-to-genital sex. There are antiviral drugs that can be used to treat genital herpes that make the outbreaks less severe.

Another sexually transmitted disease caused by a virus is AIDS, which is caused by the human immunodeficiency virus. HIV is most commonly passed from one person to another through sex or by sharing needles or syringes with a person who injects drugs and has HIV. The virus can also be passed from a mother to her baby before the baby is born, during birth, or when the baby is breastfed after birth. The difference between HIV and other viruses is that it attacks the body's immune system, destroying a type of white blood cell the body needs to fight disease. People with the virus can be treated with anti-HIV medications to keep them healthy.

A third STD-causing virus is the human papillomavirus (HPV). There are more than thirty subtypes of HPV that infect the genital area. Although the body sometimes naturally fights off the virus, some of these subtypes may cause a person to develop genital warts or cervical cancer. The HPV subtype that causes genital warts is different from the subtype that causes cervical cancer. These subtypes bring on different symptoms and require their own treatments.

STD Prevention

Both viral and bacterial STDs are passed from person to person through sexual contact. The only sure way to keep these infectious bacteria and viruses from getting into your body is not to have sex. Being in a long-term, monogamous relationship —such as a marriage—with one person who has been tested and is known not to be infected is another way to avoid getting an STD. Being faithful to your partner, and having a partner who is faithful to you, is critical. If you are having sex

Pubic Lice

Pubic lice are parasites that can be passed from one person to another through sexual contact. Commonly called crabs because of the way the parasites look when viewed up close, they can also spread through contact with infected sheets, clothing, or towels, but they are usually spread through sexual contact. These parasitic insects are usually found in the pubic hair, although they can live in the hair of the armpits, eyebrows, or beard.

Pubic lice cause itching in the genital area. A person may realize he or she has pubic lice when he or she sees lice eggs or crawling lice. In addition to itching and genital irritation, a person may see a small amount of bleeding.

The lice infestation can be treated by lotion or mousse that kills the lice. These cures can be purchased without a prescription.

Pubic lice are seen in this electron micrograph. Lice can be passed to a partner during sex.

Remaining abstinent or being in a long-term monogamous relationship are the best ways to avoid contacting STDs.

while in a relationship, it is important to remember that you are protected against STDs only if you and your partner do not have sex with others. "If you're free of infection yourself, your risk also is zero if you have sex only with one uninfected partner," notes author Charles Ebel, the former director of the Herpes Resource Center. "As soon as either partner has a new sexual contact, however, all bets are off."[65]

If you are having sex, using a condom will reduce your chances of getting an STD. A condom is a covering of latex or plastic that unrolls onto the penis. To increase the chances that it will prevent a person from getting an STD, it should be placed onto the erect penis before genital contact, and it should be removed at the end of intercourse. There is also a female condom, which is a polyurethane or latex sheath that lines the vagina. It is inserted into the vagina like a tampon.

Using a condom is not a 100 percent guarantee that a person will not get an STD, but it is a person's best protection. Using a condom is recommended if a person engages in sexual intercourse. "The only way to prevent getting STDs is to not have sex," notes physician Suzanne Swanson. "If [people] choose to be sexually active, condoms are the best we have."[66]

Although it is the best protection available against getting an STD, a condom is not without its limitations. It offers very good protection against getting a bacterial STD such as gonorrhea or chlamydia. However, it is not as good at offering complete protection against an STD that is spread through a sore or lesion on the skin, as it might not cover the area that can cause an STD infection. For example, a condom only protects against syphilis when the infected area or the site of potential exposure is protected or covered. Syphilis sores can occur in areas that are not covered by a condom. HPV can also be present throughout a person's genital area, not only in the place covered by a condom. The herpesvirus is another STD that can be spread from one person to another even though a condom is used, as the area shedding the virus may not be covered. Despite its limitations, however, a person is advised to use a condom if engaging in sexual intercourse. "They are not perfect but they're much better than nothing," Berman says. "They may not work as well for every infection, but for every infection they're much better than nothing."[67]

To increase their effectiveness, condoms need to be used both consistently and correctly. According to the American Social Health Association, correctly using a condom means using a new condom every time, and not using it with an oil-based lubricant. Condoms should not be stored in a wallet or other warm place. A person should be careful not to tear a condom when opening the wrapper and should not use fingernails or teeth to open it. If you tear a condom while opening the wrapper, the condom should be thrown away. The condom should be put on before contact with a partner's genitals, and a water-based lubricant such as K-Y Brand Jelly (but not an oil-based product such as hand lotion or petroleum jelly) should be used to keep the condom from tearing. Before use, the condom's package should be checked for an expiration date. "Old condoms can be dry, brittle or weakened and can break more easily,"[68] the American Social Health Association notes.

Denying the Problem

Young people may underestimate the risk of getting an STD or think that it is not a big deal to have one because treatments are available, says Anthony L. Contreras, who is HIV-positive and works in HIV education and prevention. They do not understand how having an STD could change their life. "That's the difficult part, trying to make them see there still is risk involved,"[69] Contreras says.

A couple reads a condom information leaflet. Condoms need to be used consistently and correctly to be effective.

Sometimes it takes getting an STD to make a teen realize that he or she is no different from anyone else and has as much chance as anyone of getting an STD. The feeling of invulnerability persists until the teen faces the consequences of his or her behavior. "For the STD-positive students I've sat with, sometimes it's the first wakeup call that I'm not Superman,"[70] says Cohen.

No-Consequences Images

It is easy to be lulled into thinking that sex has no consequences by the images of sex portrayed on television and elsewhere in the media. The characters on television shows aimed at teens are rarely shown using condoms or dealing with gonorrhea or herpes. A study by the journal *Pediatrics* found that teens who are exposed to sexual content in the movies, on television, in music and magazines were twice as likely to have sex by age sixteen. An idealized image of sex may contribute heavily to the spread of STDs. "I think the biggest problem is the huge amount of our society's media attention on how fun and cool and flashy sex is, and with all of that you almost never see negative outcomes,"[71] says physician Jill Grimes.

Confusing sex for love is another issue that can cause a teen to engage in unprotected sex, Cohen notes. A girl may feel pressured to have sex in order to please her boyfriend and keep from losing him. Teens need to have the self-respect to say no to sex and understand that sex is not a way to find love, Cohen explains. "They think if I say no to my boyfriend, he'll find another girl who will say yes," she says. "It's important to understand the difference between sex and love and how to communicate with a partner."[72]

Fighting STD Myths

Sometimes misinformation is responsible for the spread of sexually transmitted diseases. It is a misconception that birth-control methods also protect a person from STDs. Although a condom does reduce a person's chances of getting an STD, a woman is not protected from an STD by taking birth-control pills, by using a diaphragm, or by using other birth-control methods.

Some teens also mistakenly believe that "serial monogamy" will protect them from STDs. Some teens feel safe having unprotected sex with someone they are seeing exclusively. Yet it is important to realize that when you have sex with one person, you are, in effect, having sex with everyone who has ever had sex with that person. Teens are at risk for sexually transmitted diseases because of the previous sexual encounters of their partners. According to physician Lisa Marr:

> Some people, particularly teenagers, believe that having sex with only one person at a time, even if it is only for a few weeks at a time, will prevent them from becoming infected with an STD, and that it is therefore safe not to use condoms. This practice, called "serial monogamy," does not offer any protection against getting an STD since any partner could be infected with an STD from a previous relationship and not know it.[73]

Unknowingly Passing It On

Another reason that STDs continue to spread is because many people do not realize they have them and do not seek treatment. They may pass an STD onto another person without even realizing they are infected with one. An STD often shows no symptoms, and unless a person is tested, it is impossible to tell if he or she has the disease. "Most of the infections people get don't cause symptoms," Berman notes. "And the fact that you don't have any overt symptoms, or your partner has no symptoms, should be no reassurance. The great majority of STDs are probably transferred by people who have no symptoms and didn't know they had it."[74]

It is important for a sexually active person to be tested for STDs so treatment can begin if he or she is infected. Teens are not typically tested for STDs during a routine exam; however, if they are sexually active, they should talk to their doctor about the tests. Although this can be a difficult topic to bring up, doctors understand that teens may be embarrassed or ashamed about having sex and reluctant to tell their parents if they suspect they have an STD.

Talking It Over

Doctors are nonjudgmental when it comes to treating their patients. And even when those patients have STDs, the physician's only concern is to cure the disease or help make it more manageable. In some states, parents do not need to be notified of a positive STD test. A teen can be tested and treated at a Planned Parenthood clinic and pay cash so the information does not show up on an insurance statement. There are clinics specializing in treating STDs that a teen can use if he or she is not comfortable talking to a family physician. "Any underage kid who thinks they have an STD absolutely has the right to be tested,"[75] Grimes says.

If a teen wants to tell his or her parents about the STD, a family physician can be in a good position to help. The doctor can help bring up the subject in a nonjudgmental way and help parents understand the treatment the teen needs. "Don't underestimate the tolerance and forgiveness of your parents,"[76] says Grimes.

The topic of sexually transmitted diseases can be a tough subject to discuss with parents, and it can be an equally diffi-

Talking About It

It can be difficult and uncomfortable to talk about sexually transmitted diseases with your partner. However, it is important to discuss the subject in order to protect yourself from STDs. The Centers for Disease Control and Prevention offers these suggestions for broaching the topic of sex and HIV with your partner:
- Set up a mutually convenient time to talk to your partner.
- Make sure you are in a relaxed environment so your partner does not feel pressured or cornered.
- Talk about your concerns from a personal perspective. In other words, use "I" statements instead of "you" statements, which might sound accusatory or blaming.

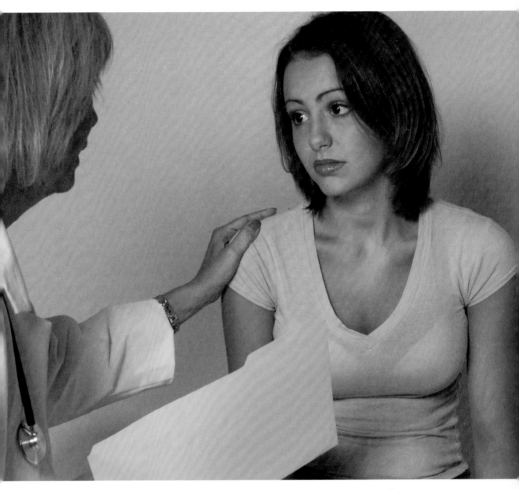

Doctors are nonjudgmental when treating their patients for an STD, so teens can feel free to talk openly about their sexual activity.

cult topic to talk about with a boyfriend or girlfriend. It is not easy, but teens should bring up the issues of protection and STD testing with any potential sex partners. A person may not be thinking about sexually transmitted diseases in the heat of the moment, but the danger is still there. Although the topic may not be easy to talk about, it is not pleasant to live with the consequences of an STD either. Being mature enough to have sex means being responsible enough to take precautions and to bring the topic of STDs out into the open.

CHAPTER FIVE

New Findings and Solutions

Because it is so important for young people to become educated about STDs, new methods of communication are being used to spread information about them. Text messaging, videos, and even online programs are being tried in order to make young people aware of the prevalence and perils of STDs. Many organizations are working to share information about the spread of these diseases, and it is hoped that education will lead to prevention.

In addition to better communication, medical advances are also helping prevent STDs. Some subtypes of HPV can now be prevented with a vaccine, and researchers are working to find new treatments for STD strains that have become resistant to some drugs. Medical advancements alone are not enough to stop the spread of the diseases, however. Preventing and treating the diseases is a critical part of curbing the spread of STDs, and educating people about them and how they are spread is an important step.

Getting the Word Out

Organizations such as the Centers for Disease Control and Prevention are working to prevent people from getting sexually transmitted diseases. The CDC is a government agency that works to help communities protect people's health by preventing

In an effort to educate youth about STDs, new methods of communications, from Web sites to blowups, like the one shown here, are being used to reach teens worldwide.

disease. The organization views the prevention of STDs as one way of keeping people healthy, and it is spreading its message about the dangers of STDs to people through health departments in large cities as well as through community groups. "To reduce the toll of STDs and protect the health of millions of Americans, expanded prevention efforts are needed,"[77] the CDC noted in a 2007 report on STDs.

Some sex education programs offer free condoms and use pamphlets to share information with teens about STD prevention and treatment.

The CDC has combined print, video, and audio materials to share information about HIV. In 2009 the Act Against AIDS campaign was launched to alert people to the infection rate of the disease and to urge them to become educated about the facts of the disease and learn how to protect themselves and others. The campaign highlights the fact that every 9.5 minutes someone becomes infected with HIV, which causes AIDS. On its Web site, www .cdc.gov/nineandahalfminutes, the facts about HIV and the people who have it are presented, along with information about prevention.

In some communities, peer education is being used to help young people get the right information about STDs. As part of his job at a Los Angeles treatment center, Anthony Contreras holds weekly meetings where he educates young people about HIV and other STDs. "The way I explain it to them is that we're in a war with diseases going on out there," he says. "Think of me as a general and you're soldiers; there's no way I would send you out there without arming you with education." He encourages young leaders in the community to attend the sessions, and he arms them with facts they in turn can pass on to their friends and family. He notes that the class is designed to be more relaxed and attention-grabbing than one in a school setting. "Here it's a loose atmosphere, so they feel comfortable," Contreras says. "We're very frank and honest and use language and terminology they'll understand."[78]

Other organizations are using Internet-based campaigns to reach young people with information about STDs. Planned Parenthood partnered with MTV and used Internet videos to emphasize the fact that young people need to get tested for sexually transmitted diseases during its Get Yourself Tested (GYT) campaign that began in 2009. Celebrities such as Soulja Boy, Flo Rida, and Perez Hilton emphasized the importance of STD testing. To reach teens, the GYT campaign began spread-

The group We Have Band performs at the tenth anniversary of MTV's Staying Alive HIV/AIDS/Safe Sex Campaign, which has proved successful in combating STDs in a number of countries.

ing the message on television and on social networking Web sites such as Facebook and Twitter. The initiative, also sponsored by the Kaiser Family Foundation, aimed to reduce the embarrassment teens feel about getting tested for STDs and make it easy for them to find a testing location. To make it simple to find a testing location, information was made available via text messaging, and teens could also search an Internet site by zip code to find a testing site near them. "Really the purpose of the GYT campaign is to generate some conversation and to start removing some of the stigma [around testing and STDs],"[79] says Cecile Richards, the president of the Planned Parenthood Federation of America.

Only a few months after the aggressive campaign to reach people under age twenty-five started, success was noted. Thousands of people searched for the campaign on the Internet and watched its YouTube videos. Testing for gonorrhea and chlamydia increased in many areas, and the number of men and women tested for HIV also increased. "We know we've found an innovative tool to reach teens and young people in a way that they will listen, learn, and, then, make healthy choices,"[80] Richards says.

Early Treatment

In addition to educating people about what STDs are and the infections they cause, the campaigns also carry a message about the importance of getting tested and treated for STDs. Getting people tested and treated is an important part of stopping the spread of STDs. Antibiotics easily treat chlamydia, gonorrhea, and syphilis. Treating these STDs and controlling their spread may also be a way to help control the spread of HIV because a person who has an STD is more susceptible to contracting HIV.

Annual tests for chlamydia are recommended for all sexually active women under age twenty-six. Although this test is recommended, it is not routinely done; thus, a woman may have to ask her health care provider about it. "We have a big push to encourage young women to be tested regularly for chlamydia, but it hasn't yet become normal; it's not an accepted medical practice like getting a Pap is," notes Berman. "Some women get the test, some don't, some get it erratically."[81]

Women are routinely screened for cervical cancer with a Pap test, which looks for abnormal, potentially cancerous cells in the cervix. In addition, it is recommended that women over age thirty be tested for HPV, which can cause cervical cancer. In women under thirty, the virus usually goes away on its own before it causes problems such as cancer. Women over thirty who have the virus, however, may have a more persistent infection that may cause cervical cancer. A woman over thirty who tests positive for HPV may need to have other tests to determine what action needs to be taken.

The Importance of Chlamydia Screening

Women who are sexually active should be screened for the STD chlamydia in order to avert a serious complication it can cause. Chlamydia can lead to a woman getting pelvic inflammatory disorder (PID). This affliction can lead to infertility or tubal pregnancy.

The Centers for Disease Control and Prevention recommends that all women who are sexually active and under twenty-six years old be screened for chlamydia. Women who are older should be screened if they have new sex partners or sex with multiple partners.

Screening women for chlamydia reduces PID cases by 50 percent, a study notes. A woman is typically not tested for chlamydia during a routine physical, but she can request that a doctor test for chlamydia. "Increased screening efforts are critical to preventing the serious health consequences of this infection," the Centers for Disease Control and Prevention notes, "particularly infertility."

Centers for Disease Control and Prevention, "Trends in Reportable Sexually Transmitted Diseases in the United States, 2007." www.cdc.gov/std/stats07/trends.htm.

Expedited Treatment

A person who tests positive for an STD and is treated should also make sure that his or her sex partner is treated for the disease; otherwise, reinfection is possible. This can be difficult, however, if that partner is not showing symptoms. Men who show no symptoms of having an STD can be especially reluctant to take the time to seek treatment and pay for a visit to a doctor. "The real problem is getting the guys treated,"[82] says Swanson.

Sometimes a girl can help her boyfriend get treatment for an STD through a practice called expedited partner therapy. To stop the spread of chlamydia, some states allow a person diagnosed with the disease to give medication to her partner if he is not allergic to the medication. This allows the partner to get treated for the disease without having to take the time to make an appointment with a doctor or even visit a clinic.

This system allows both people in a relationship to be treated for an STD, but it is controversial because a physician is treating a patient whom he or she is not seeing. In addition, there is also the question of who should pay for the medication. For these reasons, the practice is not universally accepted. However, it can be an effective way of stopping the spread of a disease, Berman notes. "From a public health perspective, we want to get the guy treated," he says. "The simplest and most efficient way is to have his partner carry the pill home and have him take it. It's very safe and very effective. It's cheap, efficient, and it helps public health."[83]

Medical Advances

In addition to encouraging people to get tested and treated, and finding ways to get medication to the infected people, work is also being done to find better ways to diagnose, treat, and prevent STDs. Although tests and treatments are available, researchers are looking for more efficient and effective ones. In addition, researchers are also looking for new ways to prevent the spread of STDs.

One recently developed vaccine now available is the Gardasil vaccine. It protects young women against two subtypes of

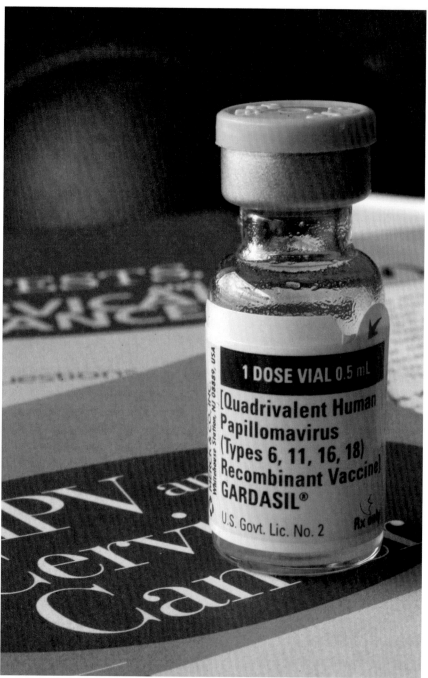

The recently developed Gardasil vaccine protects women against two subtypes of HPV that can cause cervical cancer.

HPV that cause cervical cancer and two subtypes that cause genital warts. The vaccine offers protection against the two HPV subtypes that cause 70 percent of cervical cancer cases. It also protects against the two subtypes that cause 90 percent of genital warts. The vaccine is recommended for girls eleven and twelve years old, who get the vaccine in a series of three injections. The injections are given over a six-month period, with the second and third doses given at two and six months after the first. The vaccines are recommended for young girls because Gardasil works best when it is given before a girl has contact with the types of HPV that Gardasil prevents.

Other prevention efforts include research work on other vaccines and topical microbicides, which would be used to prevent STD infection in different ways. A vaccine would be given as an injection and would be expected to provide long-term protection against an STD such as herpes, HIV, or types of HPV. Topical microbicides that would prevent STDs would be applied before sexual intercourse and could be in the form of a gel or cream. The topical microbicides would not offer long-term protection and would need to be reapplied.

So far, research has produced mixed results with STD vaccines. Although HPV vaccines are effective, scientists have not yet been able to develop a vaccine that offers protection against herpes or HIV. Topical microbicides are being studied, but products have not yet been approved for use. Research is being done to see if they can protect a person against HIV, but that research has not yet yielded a product that is on the market.

Both STD vaccines and topical microbicides are not without controversy. Some people have a moral objection to protecting people against sexually transmitted diseases. They feel that vaccinating people against the diseases would condone sex outside of marriage and promiscuity.

In addition to working to improve STD prevention, researchers are also looking into new ways to treat STDs. For example, scientists are studying gonorrhea and its ability to become resistant to some treatments. Because HIV also becomes resistant to medication, new treatments are being developed for it. Under the HIV Prevention Trials Network, a worldwide collaboration of clinical trials, researchers look for safe and efficient ways to prevent the transmission of HIV.

Honest Communication

Researchers and organizations are working to reduce the number of people who become infected with sexually transmitted diseases, but they need support from the public. There are steps that everyone can take to slow the spread of these infections. Communication, however, is perhaps the most important step of all, particularly when it is between parents and children, boyfriends and girlfriends, and teachers and students.

Couples should talk about their HIV status and their history of STDs, and they should know the importance of regular testing. If you find you have an STD, it is important to let the person you got it from know that you have tested positive. "You absolutely need to tell the person you got it from," notes physician Jill Grimes. "Because these diseases are silent, you need to recognize that there's a significant chance the person you got it from did not know they had it." If you can't bring yourself to talk to an ex-boyfriend or ex-girlfriend about it, there are

A billboard promoting abstinence in Baltimore sends a message to teens. Abstinence is a sure way to prevent STDs.

Abstinence Vows Are Often Broken

Teens in Britain line up to take the abstinence vow. A person can avoid contracting an STD by abstaining from sex.

Teens who sign a virginity pledge and vow to abstain from sex before marriage often break that pledge, a study indicates. A 2009 study published in *Pediatrics* by Janet Rosenbaum indicates that teens who signed a virginity pledge were just as likely to have taken part in sexual behavior as teens who did not sign a pledge. They were also less likely to use condoms to protect themselves against STDs or use birth control than teens who had not signed a pledge.

"Virginity pledges may not affect sexual behavior," the study concluded, "but may decrease the likelihood of taking precautions during sex. Clinicians should provide birth control information to all adolescents, especially virginity pledgers."

Janet Rosenbaum, "Patient Teenagers? A Comparison of the Sexual Behavior of Virginity Pledgers and Matched Nonpledgers," *Pediatrics*, January 2009, p. 110. http://pediatrics .aappublications.org/cgi/content/full/123/1/e110.

e-cards available on the CDC Web site that can be sent to alert someone that you have been exposed and encourage them to be tested. "You have to take some ownership of this," Grimes says. "You made an adult choice."[84]

The decision to have sex is a serious one, and the possibility of catching an STD is a very real consideration for anyone considering entering into a sexual relationship. The signs and symptoms of an infection may not be present, but that does not mean it cannot cause serious damage in the future.

Millions of people are currently infected with STDs. In order for those numbers to fall, it is essential that people get tested, treated, and realize the risk that sexual activity carries. Abstaining from sex or being in a long-term monogamous relationship with someone who is not infected are the only sure ways to avoid getting an STD. Although a condom reduces the chances that a person will become infected, a sexually active person should be aware of the implications of that decision. "Sex must not be taken trivially," notes Stuart Berman. "It's an important decision. People need to be thinking that every time they have sex there's that risk. We don't want everybody to stay in their own caves, but you don't know who the person is who's going to end up having a pretty bad problem with it."[85]

Notes

Introduction: Could It Happen to You?

1. Susan Cohen, telephone interview by author, April 24, 2009.
2. Cohen, interview.
3. Stuart Berman, telephone interview by author, May 1, 2009.

Chapter One: A Significant Problem

4. National Institute of Allergy and Infectious Diseases, "Sexually Transmitted Infections." www3.niaid.nih.gov/topics/sti/.
5. Quoted in Daniel J. DeNoon, "Chlamydia, STD Rates Soar in U.S.," MedicineNet, November 13, 2007. http://medicine net.com/script/main/art.asp?articlekey-85217.
6. Centers for Disease Control and Prevention, "Trends in Reportable Sexually Transmitted Diseases in the United States, 2007." www.cdc.gov/std/stats07/trends.htm.
7. Centers for Disease Control and Prevention, "Trends in Reportable Sexually Transmitted Diseases in the United States, 2007."
8. Cohen, interview.
9. Quoted in DeNoon, "Chlamydia, STD Rates Soar in U.S."
10. Berman, interview.
11. Suzanne Swanson, telephone interview by author, April 14, 2009.
12. Centers for Disease Control and Prevention, "Trends in Reportable Sexually Transmitted Diseases in the United States, 2007."
13. Centers for Disease Control and Prevention, "Trends in Reportable Sexually Transmitted Diseases in the United States, 2007."
14. American Cancer Society, "Overview: Cervical Cancer. What Causes Cancer of the Cervix?" www.cancer.org/doc root/CRI/content/CRI_2_2_2X_What_causes_cancer_of_the _cervix_Can_it_be_prevented_8.asp?sitearea=.

15. Jill Grimes, telephone interview by author, April 14, 2009.
16. Grimes, interview.
17. Anthony L. Contreras, telephone interview by author, April 17, 2009.
18. Grimes, interview.
19. Maria, telephone interview by author, April 12, 2009.
20. Berman, interview.
21. Michelle Landry, telephone interview by author, April 21, 2009.
22. Cohen, interview.

Chapter Two: Diagnosis, Testing, and Treatment

23. Lisa Marr, *Sexually Transmitted Diseases: A Physician Tells You What You Need to Know*. Baltimore: Johns Hopkins University Press, 2007, p. 153.
24. Marr, *Sexually Transmitted Diseases*, p. 36.
25. Marr, *Sexually Transmitted Diseases*, p. 291.
26. Grimes, interview.
27. Berman, interview.
28. Berman, interview.

Chapter Three: People Living with STDs

29. Maria, interview.
30. Maria, interview.
31. Maria, interview.
32. Maria, interview.
33. Maria, interview.
34. Maria, interview.
35. Maria, interview.
36. Maria, interview.
37. Kelly, telephone interview by author, April 2009.
38. Kelly, interview.
39. Kelly, interview.
40. Kelly, interview.
41. Kelly, interview.
42. Kelly, interview.
43. Kelly, interview.

44. Michelle, telephone interview by author, April 2009.
45. Michelle, interview.
46. Michelle, interview.
47. Michelle, interview.
48. Michelle, interview.
49. Michelle, interview.
50. Michelle, interview.
51. Contreras, interview.
52. Contreras, interview.
53. Contreras, interview.
54. Contreras, interview.
55. Contreras, interview.
56. Contreras, interview.
57. Contreras, interview.
58. Contreras, interview.
59. Contreras, interview.
60. Tom, telephone interview by author, June 11, 2009.
61. Tom, interview.
62. Tom, interview.

Chapter Four: Causes and Prevention

63. Cohen, interview.
64. Berman, interview.
65. Charles Ebel, *Managing Herpes*. Triangle Park, NC: American Social Health Association, 1998, p. 183.
66. Swanson, interview.
67. Berman, interview.
68. American Social Health Association, "How to Use a Condom." www.ashastd.org/condom/condom_overview.cfm.
69. Contreras, interview.
70. Cohen, interview.
71. Grimes, interview.
72. Cohen, interview.
73. Marr, *Sexually Transmitted Diseases*, p. 86.
74. Berman, interview.
75. Grimes, interview.
76. Grimes, interview.

Chapter Five: New Findings and Solutions

77. Centers for Disease Control and Prevention, "Trends in Reportable Sexually Transmitted Diseases in the United States, 2007."

78. Contreras, interview.

79. Quoted in Frank Washkuch, "MTV, Planned Parenthood Collaborate on STD Awareness," April 13, 2009. www.pr weekus.com/MTV-Planned-Parenthood-collaborate-on-STD-awareness/article/130372/.

80. Quoted in Planned Parenthood, "MTV's GYT Campaign Spurs Nationwide Movement to 'Get Yourself Tested.'" www.plannedparenthood.org/about-us/news room/press-releases/mtvs-gyt-campaign-spurs-nationwide-movement-get-yourself-tested-27926.htm.

81. Berman, interview.

82. Swanson, interview.

83. Berman, interview.

84. Grimes, interview.

85. Berman, interview.

Glossary

abstinence: Making a choice not to have sex.

acquired immunodeficiency syndrome (AIDS): A life-threatening condition caused by the human immunodeficiency virus (HIV). HIV damages the immune system, making a person susceptible to some infections and cancers.

bacteria: Single-celled organism visible only under a microscope. Some bacteria cause infection, but others are beneficial.

chlamydia: A common sexually transmitted disease caused by bacteria. It spreads easily and is curable.

condom: A thin covering made of latex or polyurethane that fits over the penis.

fallopian tubes: The part of a woman's reproductive system that transports the egg from the ovary to the uterus.

genital herpes: A sexually transmitted disease caused by a virus that causes blisters, usually in the genital area.

genitals: A person's sex organs.

gonorrhea: A common sexually transmitted disease. It is caused by bacteria.

herpes simplex virus: A viral infection mainly affecting the mouth or genital area. Herpes simplex virus type 1 (HSV-1) is usually associated with an infection of the mouth. Herpes simplex virus type 2 (HSV-2) is typically associated with genital sores.

human immunodeficiency virus (HIV): The virus that causes acquired immunodeficiency syndrome (AIDS).

human papillomavirus (HPV): A virus with many subtypes that can cause genital warts or cervical cancer.

parasite: An organism that lives in or on another organism.

syphilis: A sexually transmitted disease caused by bacteria. It progresses through several stages and, if left untreated, can lead to blindness, mental problems, and death.

tubal pregnancy: A pregnancy in which the fertilized egg implants in a woman's fallopian tube rather than in the uterus.

uterus: An organ in a woman's reproductive system where the fetus grows; it is also called the womb.

virus: Microscopic organisms that live and reproduce inside host cells and are the cause of infectious diseases.

Organizations to Contact

American Social Health Association (ASHA)
PO Box 13827
Research Triangle Park, NC 27709
phone: (919) 361-8400
STI Resource Center Hotline: (800) 227-8922
fax: (919) 361-8425
Web site: www.ashastd.org

The ASHA offers accurate and reliable information about sexually transmitted infections. The nonprofit organization, founded in 1914, works to improve public health as it focuses on STDs. Its publications include patient educational materials such as a quarterly newsletter about herpes treatment and research as well as pamphlets, books, and fact sheets on a variety of topics relating to STDs.

Centers for Disease Control and Prevention (CDC)
1600 Clifton Rd.
Atlanta, GA 30333
phone: (800) CDC-INFO (232-4636)
e-mail: cdcinfo@cdc.gov
Web site: www.cdc.gov

The CDC is the top public health agency in the United States. Part of the U.S. Department of Health and Human Services, it focuses on the prevention and control of disease, injury, and disability in order to protect people's health and promote quality of life. It responds to health threats and offers information on a wide variety of diseases and health-related topics. Information and brochures about specific sexually transmitted diseases can be found on its Web site.

National Institute of Allergy and Infectious Diseases
6610 Rockledge Dr., MSC 6612
Bethesda, MD 20892-6612
phone: (866) 284-4107 or (301) 496-5717
fax: (301) 402-3573
Web site: www.niaid.nih.gov

This organization conducts and supports research into infectious diseases as well as allergic diseases. It is part of the U.S. Department of Health and Human Services and the National Institutes of Health. Its research has led to new treatments, vaccines, and tests. It publishes free pamphlets about topics including the immune system and vaccines as well as fact sheets about chlamydia, genital herpes, gonorrhea, and other STDs.

National Prevention Information Network (NPIN)
PO Box 6003
Rockville, MD 20849-6003
phone: (800) 458-5231
fax: (333) 282-7681
e-mail: info@cdcnpin.org
Web site: www.cdcnpin.org

As the information service for the CDC, the NPIN distributes information about sexually transmitted diseases and other diseases. In addition to producing materials, it also catalogs and collects information that can be shared and used by people working in fields related to those diseases. It has databases of educational materials as well as fact sheets, guidelines, reports, and brochures that can be ordered.

National Women's Health Information Center
8270 Willow Oaks Corporate Dr.
Fairfax, VA 22031
phone: (800) 994-9662 or (888) 220-5446
Web site: www.womenshealth.gov

A service of the Office on Women's Health in the U.S. Department of Health and Human Services, this organization advocates the health and well-being of women. It promotes health equity for women and girls through programs, education of health professionals, and health information for consumers. Its free publications answer frequently asked questions about sexually transmitted diseases and other health concerns.

Planned Parenthood Federation of America
434 W. Thirty-third St.
New York, NY 10001
phone: (212) 541-7800 or (800) 230-7526
fax: (212) 245-1845
Web site: www.plannedparenthood.org

This organization offers information on sexual and reproductive health care. It operates more than 850 health centers nationwide and offers testing and treatment for sexually transmitted diseases. It also provides sex education, offering information about STD prevention. Through its online store, found at www.ppfastore.org, it offers a number of brochures on sexual health.

For Further Reading

Books

Jill Grimes, *Seductive Delusions: How Everyday People Catch STDs*. Baltimore: Johns Hopkins University Press, 2008. Grimes delivers the facts on sexually transmitted diseases by looking at them through the eyes of characters infected with them.

Miranda Hunter, *Staying Safe: A Teen's Guide to Sexually Transmitted Diseases*. Philadelphia: Mason Crest, 2005. This book provides information on sexually transmitted diseases, including how to stay safe and get help.

Tassia Kolesnikow, *Sexually Transmitted Diseases*. San Diego: Lucent, 2004. This work looks at the concerns of STDs as well as prevention, diagnosis, and treatment.

Lisa Marr, *Sexually Transmitted Diseases*. Baltimore: Johns Hopkins University Press, 2007. Marr provides detailed information on more than twenty STDs.

Web Sites

Centers for Disease Control and Prevention (www .cdc.gov). A government Web site with information about the infection rates for sexually transmitted diseases as well as their causes and treatment options.

National Institute of Allergy and Infectious Diseases (www.niaid.nih.gov). This site provides news and information on disease research.

Office on Women's Health (www.womenshealth.gov). A Web site from the U.S. Department of Health and Human Services that offers information on how sexually transmitted diseases are spread, their symptoms, testing, and treatment.

Planned Parenthood (www.plannedparenthood.org). This site provides information on sexual health, including clinic locations where teens can get tested for sexually transmitted diseases.

Index

Picture Credits

About the Author

Terri Dougherty has written more than seventy books for young people. As the mother of three teens, she sees the value of education about sexually transmitted diseases.